The Noah's Ark *by Susan Barger. Machine appliquéd printed and plain cottons, 90" x 72". Because of its thickness, this quilt was tied rather than top-stitched. The tying, which holds the layers together, is beautifully incorporated into the total design.*

The Oregon Quilt. *Appliqué, 102" x 96". Twenty-one women created this unique quilt that depicts historical and geographical Oregon scenes in the tradition of the nineteenth century "album" or "presentation" quilt. Each woman chose a personally meaningful subject, and the quilt, a true labor of love, took about a year to complete. Photo courtesy of Helen Bitar.*

Untitled *by Pat Butler. Batik on cotton. In this sculptural piece, various parts of the figure were outlined with stitching and then stuffed from the back.*

CREATIVE QUILTING

CREATIVE QUILTING

BY ELSA BROWN

WATSON-GUPTILL PUBLICATIONS, NEW YORK

PITMAN PUBLISHING, LONDON

Copyright © 1975 by Watson-Guptill Publications

First published 1975 in the United States and Canada by Watson-Guptill Publications,
a division of Billboard Publications, Inc.,
One Astor Plaza, New York, N.Y. 10036

Library of Congress Cataloging in Publication Data
Brown, Elsa, 1930-
  Creative quilting.
  Bibliography: p.
  Includes index.
  1. Quilting. I. Title.
TT835.B73 1975   746.4'6   74-34282
ISBN 0-8230-1105-4

Published in Great Britain by Sir Isaac Pitman & Sons Ltd.,
39 Parker Street, London WC2B 5PB
ISBN 0-273-00911-7

Manufactured in U.S.A.

First Printing, 1975
Second Printing, 1976

Edited by Jennifer Place
Designed by Bob Fillie
Set in 10 point Century by Harold Black Inc.

For Bill

Contents

Patchwork 31

Appliqué 51

Printed, Painted, and Dyed Fabrics 115

Ideas and Design 127

Acknowledgments

My deepest thanks and appreciation goes to the many artists who so generously shared their ideas and allowed their works to be represented in the book. I also wish to thank the museums and galleries who promptly answered my requests for photographs and provided many valuable suggestions as well. I am especially grateful to Bob Hanson for his excellent photos and tireless good humor, and to Sharron Hedges for her perception and skill in rendering the drawings. My thanks also to Vesta Vetter who started it all when she taught me how to do trapunto. I am also grateful to my husband, Bill, and my children, Jeff, Jordan, Alison, and Brenda, for their patience, help, and encouragement—not only on this project but through the years.

Introduction

New York Beauty, *69" x 89". Cotton pieced quilt, mid-nineteenth century. This very old pattern dates from 1776 and was extremely popular for many years. The "fans" are pieced first, and then the dividing borders are pieced in strips. Blocks are formed with four fans and the plain white area, and the entire quilt is assembled. Photo courtesy of the Shelburne Museum, Inc., Vermont.*

QUILTING IS THE age-old craft of decoratively stitching together two layers of fabric—usually with a soft, thick filler sandwiched between them. The stitching is not only practical, but provides unlimited opportunities for artistic expression.

The actual quilting process can be divided into two basic techniques. In the first and oldest form, two pieces of cloth—a top and a lining—are held together with stitching to produce what is called "flat quilting." If a thick inner padding is inserted between the top and the backing, the result is known as "wadded quilting" in England, or sometimes "English quilting." In America we do not have a specific term for common quilting, but the term "padded quilting" is gaining popularity as it describes the process and distinguishes it from other stuffing techniques.

The second basic type of quilting reverses the procedure of the first type. First the design is stitched by hand or machine through the two layers of cloth, and then the stuffing is inserted into the areas defined by the stitching through openings punched or cut in the backing. This method is called "trapunto," meaning "to punch through" in Italian. When the design consists of narrow parallel bands of stitching that are stuffed by threading them with yarn or cord, the result is called "Italian quilting" or "cord-quilting." In trapunto and cord-quilting, the design is raised from the background for a richly sculptural relief effect.

Often a quilted object is identified by what has been done to the top, or outermost layer, rather than the specific padding technique. In the United States, especially, the word "quilt" almost always conjures up an image of the traditional pieced or appliquéd top rather than the layering and stitching that is the actual quilting. The construction and embellishment of the quilt top gives the quilt its identity and expresses the imagination and originality of the artist. This book will cover each of the main methods of top construction and decoration: patchwork, appliqué, and painted, printed, and dyed fabrics.

While the basic quilting techniques have remained unchanged for thousands of years, the forms of expression have changed drastically in recent times. Fabric has become an important sculptural medium for relief as well as three-dimensional forms. Many artists who formerly worked with more traditional materials have turned to cloth to create imaginative wall hangings, dolls, sculptural objects, and body coverings as well as functional bed coverings and accessories for the home. Sometimes traditional examples of quilting or patchwork provide inspiration or points of departure, but as often as not, the contemporary artist is not even aware that what he is doing is quilting. This book will present the basic traditional techniques of quilting and patchwork, as well as the imaginative application of these techniques in contemporary work.

Tools and Materials

Using a Hoop. *A large wooden embroidery hoop is used to lap-quilt an antique top. The left hand is placed under the hoop to help guide the needle along.*

*Q*UILTING HAS ESCAPED the boundaries of tradition in recent years to such an extent that it is often barely recognizable as quilting. Yet, the tools of today are the same as those of long ago. The basic sewing supplies—needles, pins, thread, scissors, tape measure, etc.—are as close as your household sewing basket or neighborhood variety store. Materials or pieces of equipment that are unavailable locally can be ordered by mail or, as in the case of the quilting frame, made at home. Art supply stores are a good source for dyes, textile paints, brushes, tracing paper, and other supplies not related to sewing.

The following discussion will deal with supplies that are basic to a variety of quilting techniques. Tools and materials that are needed for specific techniques, such as trapunto, patchwork, appliqué, will be discussed in the chapters that cover those techniques.

Remember, what works well for one person will not necessarily work for another. By experimenting and keeping an open mind, you will soon settle on the tools and materials that are most comfortable for you.

Tools

The following tools are basic to all types of quilting techniques. Most of these can be purchased in department stores, five-and-dimes, or sewing supply stores.

Needles and Pins. You should have an assortment of sewing needles on hand as it is often difficult to determine in advance the exact size needle you will need for a given job.

For actual quilting, you will need a quilting needle, which is a short, sharp needle about an inch long. A slightly longer needle, called a "between," is also good for quilting. Choose either a #8 or #9. For trapunto you will also need a large-eyed blunt needle, sometimes called a yarn needle or bodkin.

Glass-headed pins are preferable to dressmaker's pins although they cost a bit more. They are larger and therefore easier to pin through layers of batting and cloth.

Scissors. Sharp, accurate dressmaker's shears are a must for quiltmaking, especially for cutting out patchwork pieces. Small, sharp-pointed embroidery scissors are useful for trapunto and also for snipping threads.

Thread. There is a confusing array of threads on the market, and again, you should experiment and then stay with what works best for you. Quilting thread, when it is available, usually comes only in white or a very limited color range. It is nice to have for actual quilting as it is stronger and smoother than most other thread.

If you cannot find quilting thread, heavy-duty mercerized cotton thread, #50 or #60, is an excellent substitute and comes in a wide color range. Don't confuse "heavy-duty" with "extra-strong" button and carpet thread, which

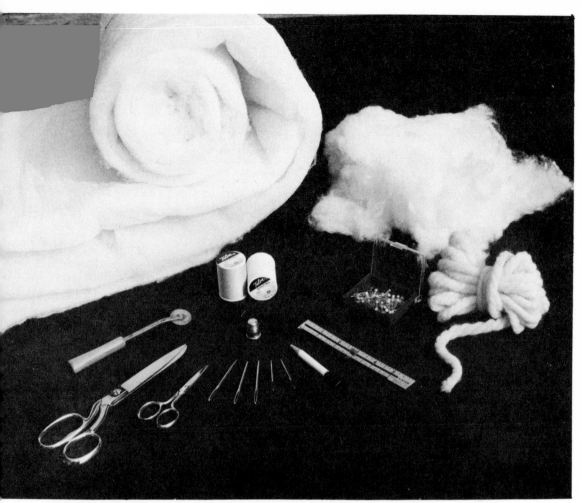

Materials and tools. *Some of the items used for quilting are dacron batting, polyester fiberfill, a tracing wheel, shears, embroidery scissors, blunt needles, bulky yarn, quilting thread, pins, a hem gauge, and a thimble.*

is visibly thicker. Pure cotton thread is becoming hard to find as it is fast being replaced by polyester and cotton-wrapped polyester fibers. While the synthetics are excellent for dressmaking and for straight seams, they are not suited to hand sewing because of their tendency to knot, twist, and fray. This can sometimes be alleviated, however, by drawing the thread through a chunk of beeswax before sewing with it.

Thimble. Even if you do not use a thimble for ordinary sewing, you will need one for quilting because of the thickness of the layers of fabric. It should fit your middle finger.

Pencils, Markers, and Chalk. You will need a medium-hard drawing pencil for sketching, transferring designs, and for marking around templates. Felt markers can be useful for freehand designing and for planning patchwork blocks in color.

Chalk is messy, but it is generally safer to use than pencil if you are drawing a design on the right side of a fabric. It can later be brushed off with a soft brush. Chalk pencils are useful for fine lines and for drawing on dark fabrics.

Paper. Sheets of butcher paper, newsprint, or shelf paper can be taped together for laying out patterns for large quilting designs.

For tracing designs you can use sheets of tissue paper, or tracing paper, which is more expensive but stronger. These can also be taped together for tracing large designs.

Graph paper is useful for working out patchwork patterns, placing blocks on a quilt, and planning borders and strips.

Dressmaker's carbon paper is a transfer paper that comes in colors and does not rub off on fabrics. It is used for transferring patterns to cloth with a tracing wheel or some other blunt instrument.

Cardboard, Sandpaper, and Acetate. Quilting and patchwork templates can be made from all these materials. Sandpaper has the advantage of gripping the fabric, but the disadvantage of eventually wearing out at the edges. Cardboard also wears out. You can prolong the life of cardboard and sandpaper templates by taping the edges, but for a large project it makes more sense to start out with a more durable material. Acetate or thin plastic sheets can be purchased in art supply stores and are easily cut into long-lasting templates. Discarded plastic placemats or containers can also be used.

Measuring Tools. You will need a tape measure, yardstick, ruler, and hem gauge for the various measuring jobs concerned with quiltmaking. A see-through plastic ruler, with inches marked on the width as well as the length, is a great help in adding the seam allowance to patchwork patterns.

Hoops and Frames. A large wooden tambour embroidery hoop is excellent for quilting. It adjusts to the thickness of the quilt and can be used for lap quilting.

Ready-made quilting frames can be purchased in needlework departments of large department stores, or they can be ordered from a needlework supply shop or mail-order house. Directions for making your own simple frame from stock lumber are given in Chapter 2.

Sewing Machine. A sewing machine is a useful tool for quilting. It need not be expensive or even very new. The machine used for the demonstrations in this book is more than ten years old and is the one I use for all my creative work.

Materials

Part of the excitement of quilting today is the wide variety of fabrics available—department stores, sewing centers, even antique stores or rummage sales, all offer good hunting. See the suppliers list in the back of the book for places to order stuffing if unavailable locally.

Fillers and Stuffing. Until very recently, the most common filler available for quilting was cotton batting. Cotton is still readily available, but it has many disadvantages. The tendency to lump and shift during washing means that it must be quite closely quilted. Also, cotton tends to resist the needle during sewing and results in a relatively thin quilt.

Well-washed wool and cotton blankets have traditionally been used for filler in lightweight quilts. Today you can buy lightweight blankets made of synthetic materials that are easy to handle and retain their fluffiness after washing. Since woven materials do not lump or shift, they are good to use for filler in tied quilts, clothing, and other items that will not be closely quilted. Loose polyester stuffing, as well as feathers and down, can be used for stuffing comforters and puffs. Down comforters that have worn covers can be used for filler in tied quilts.

The best filler available is dacron batting. It comes in several thicknesses and sizes, and the layers can be pulled apart when a thinner filler is needed. Many dacron battings have a glazed surface, which makes them easy to handle and prevents lumping and shifting during washing. The glaze also prevents the fibers of the batting from working through the top fabric after the piece is quilted. Because of its fluffiness, dacron batting makes a more luxurious, puffy quilt than any other filler. For an extra-thick quilt, two layers of batting placed one on top of the other can be used.

Fabrics. Building up a collection of fabrics is not only fun, but is part of the creative process. The materials themselves will stimulate you and suggest ways of working that might not otherwise occur to you. In the beginning you will probably buy most of your materials in a fabric store, but you will seek other sources as you begin to see the possibilities in many different kinds of materials.

Remnant counters and mill-end stores are excellent sources for fabrics. If you or your friends sew at home, you can use the leftover scraps for appliqué and patchwork. Do not overlook usable parts of worn clothing or household items. Blankets, curtains, trousers, dresses, shirts, coats, suits—even underwear, stockings, and neckties—provide a variety in texture and a mellowness that cannot be found in new materials. Thrift shops or rummage and garage sales are other sources for used materials.

Obviously, the most important consideration in selecting materials for a project is how the item will be used. If the piece is to receive heavy wear and need frequent washing you will want to think twice about using worn or flimsy fabrics. All washable fabrics should be laundered before they are used to prevent bleeding and shrinkage in the finished piece. Sometimes I add a little bleach to the wash water to take the slickness out of a new fabric. This is entirely a matter of preference.

Some purists insist on using only natural materials, such as cotton, wool, silk, and linen, while to others it makes little difference. Most often you will find that you are using a combination of natural and synthetic materials, the deciding factor being color, texture, and suitability rather than fiber content.

Quilted Doll, *by Elsa Brown. Machine darning is used here to fill in the unstuffed areas of this trapunto-quilted doll.*

Basic Procedures

*Y*OU CAN LEARN TO quilt if you can thread a needle and make a simple running stitch. Even if you are a beginner, you will find that as your work progresses and you gain confidence, the basic techniques will soon become second nature. What may have begun as a simple utilitarian function soon turns into a means of self-expression.

Ideally, there should be no rigid rules or restrictions connected with creative work. There are, however, certain tried and true methods which, if you know them, can save you endless time and frustration. Knowing the right techniques and how to apply them will enable you to relax and expend your energies on the more creative aspects of a project instead.

Each method described in this chapter will effect a desired result in the completion of some task related to the making or finishing of a quilted item. Procedures that apply only to specific techniques, such as patchwork, appliqué, trapunto, etc., will be covered in detail in separate chapters.

Quilting Designs

The term quilting refers to the actual stitching together of the top, backing, and filler. Before you choose a design for the quilting stitches, you should give careful consideration to the design of the top and to how the stitches will complement it. Many quilters concentrate on the top design, while ignoring the creative potential of the actual quilting. The stitching should never be something that is imposed on the top as a strictly utilitarian device. It should merge with the design of the top by throwing the fabric surface into soft relief, and it should provide a texture and a character that will unify the whole piece.

The simplest quilting patterns can be done by eye and do not have to be marked on the fabric. In patchwork, the stitching can follow the outline of each geometric shape, either in the seam or on either side of the seam. Appliqué shapes can be accentuated by stitching around the appliquéd shape for several rows. Plain areas can be quilted with stitching that echoes the patchwork or appliqué shapes, or with stitching that exists as a separate design unit.

Plain-top quilts, in which the quilting line forms the entire design, must be carefully planned with an eye toward unity and rhythm of design. The plain-top quilt, usually white, was so highly developed in England that the term "English quilting" is still applied to any quilting of that type. The beautiful and elaborate patterns were usually developed with the aid of templates (or household objects such as plates, glasses, cups, etc.). In both England and America, tops could be sent out to be marked and even quilted if the quilter did not wish to do it herself. This was most common in England, where itinerant quilters went from village to village marking the tops as well as quilting them. Interestingly, some of the more famous markers and quilters in England were men.

English Coverlet *(detail) 1703. Here you can see the effect of fine hand stitches used as the sole means of decoration. Courtesy of the Victoria and Albert Museum, London.*

Marking the Top

If your design is too elaborate to quilt by eye, there are several ways to transfer the full-sized design from the paper to the cloth. Marking is most easily accomplished on a hard surface before the layers are stacked and before the quilt is set into the frame (if you intend to use one).

Whichever method you choose from those listed below, bear in mind that it is often difficult, if not impossible, to remove carbon and pencil markings. Even after washing or dry-cleaning, the marks may remain to spoil the work. If you must use pencil, remember that a dotted line is less visible than a solid line and is just as effective.

Dressmaker's Carbon. Select a color of carbon paper that is similar to the color of the fabric, but that contrasts enough so you can see the lines on the fabric. For a large design, you may have to tape or pin several sheets of paper together. Position the carbon face down on the fabric, pin it in place, and trace over each line with a tracing wheel or a blunt instrument.

Tracing Pencil. Trace over the lines of the design on the right side of the paper pattern with the pencil. Place the paper pattern face down on the fabric and iron. The pencil lines will be transferred onto the fabric.

Pierced Paper. Draw your design on tissue or wrapping paper. Lay this on top of the fabric and pierce the paper at regular intervals along the lines of the design with a sharp lead pencil. Another method is to pierce the paper along the lines with a heavy needle and then force chalk or stamping powder through the holes.

For machine quilting, you can pin a tissue-paper pattern to the quilt top and, following the lines of the design, stitch through all the layers at once. The tissue can easily be torn away when the stitching is completed.

Templates. A template is a pattern, traditionally made of tin or wood, that serves as a guide in drawing designs. The template is placed on the fabric, outlined with chalk or pencil, and then moved to the next position. Household objects, such as cups, plates, or coins, can also be used for templates.

Masking Tape. For straight lines, you can lay down strips of masking tape right on the fabric to use as a guide. The tape can be peeled off later.

Preparing to Quilt

Most projects can be quilted without a frame, but with or without a frame, the method of assembly is the same. The backing, or bottommost layer of the quilt, should be prepared so it is a few inches larger all around than the filler. You can seam lengths of fabric on the machine until you have the proper size, or you can use a bed sheet or extra-wide muslin. You should experiment, however, as some muslins and percales are very closely woven and therefore hard to sew through.

After the backing has been prepared, place it wrong-side up, with seams pressed open, on the floor or table and smooth it out. On top of this, place the sheet of batting or filler. Leave about 2″ of lining showing around the edge. If the batting or filler must be pieced, rather than using seams you can overlap the edges to be joined by about an inch and then baste. This will prevent an unpleasant ridge in the finished piece.

Next, place the quilt top right side up on top of the filler and smooth out all the fullness from the center to the sides. Leave about 2″ of batting showing around the edge of the top (see Figure 1).

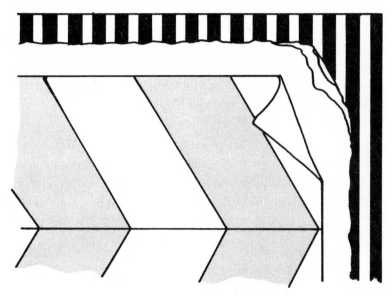

Figure 1. *The layers are stacked with the backing first, then the filler, and lastly the top. Each layer should extend a few inches beyond the one on top of it.*

You can now set the quilt into a frame or hoop, or simply begin quilting. If you decide to use a hoop, begin stitching as close to the center of the quilt as possible and smooth the fullness to the sides as you move the hoop. In any off-frame method the layers should first be profusely basted to prevent shifting. Small items, such as parts of garments, can be lap quilted, but large projects are best quilted flat on a table. If you place a piece of thick glass with taped edges, a piece of formica, or some other slick-surfaced material under the area you are stitching, it will help the needle glide along and save your table top from scratches.

The Quilting Stitch

The quilting stitch consists of lines of short, even running stitches taken with a single strand of thread in a short needle. Years ago, when great attention was paid to fine stitching, each stitch was taken in two motions. First the needle was pushed down through the three layers with one hand. Then it was caught by the other hand under the quilt and guided up again as close to the first stitch as possible. There are accounts of quilting bees in colonial times where the children were stationed under the quilting frame to catch the needle when it came through and guide it back up. Today, quilters are more concerned with the visual effects of the work and are not overly concerned with the number of stitches per inch. This does not mean, however, that you should abandon craftsmanship altogether. With practice you can learn to make an even line of stitching by taking two or three short stitches at a time before pulling the needle through. If the batting is thick it helps to take a longer stitch on the wrong side, taking care to keep the top stitches as short and even as possible.

You can begin quilting at the center of the piece and work out to the sides, or you can begin at one side and work across to the other side. It is easier to sew from right to left (left to right if you are left-handed) and toward yourself rather than away from yourself. In quilting without a frame, I prefer to start at the center as the fullness can be smoothed to the sides as the work progresses. You should check the back occasionally to make sure that no wrinkles have developed.

Beginning and Ending. To begin stitching, make a knot in the thread about an inch from the end. Insert the needle from the wrong side (the backing layer) and draw the thread gently through the layers until you can feel the knot pop through the backing and bury itself in the batting. To end off the thread, run your needle through the top layer only, going back over the last five or six stitches. Make a loop through the last stitch, insert the needle into the batting, and run it along for an inch or so. Bring the thread to the surface again and clip the end close to the quilt top.

The Quilting Frame

A quilting frame should be used when you are making a traditional pieced quilt in which blocks fit together to make up a complete design. It is also more comfortable to use a frame with any quilt that is larger than throw size.

You can buy a ready-made frame, or you can make your own simple frame from stock lumber. First, cut two pieces of 1″ x 2″ lumber that are each about a foot longer than the width of the quilt desired. Then cut two pieces that are about 3 feet long for stretchers. Wrap a strip of heavy muslin, denim, or canvas around each of the two lengths of wood, leaving one edge of the fabric projecting about 2″. Then staple or tack the fabric in place at even intervals all along the length of wood.

After you have assembled and basted the layers, lay the quilt out on the floor or table and baste the lining to the fabric strip on each end of the frame (see Figure 2). At this point you will need someone to help you roll up the quilt and attach the stretcher bars with C-clamps. Roll up each end of the quilt toward the center of the frame until about 2 feet of the quilt is left exposed. As each exposed area of the quilt is stitched, the frame is unclamped, rolled to another section, and reclamped. Proceed from the center of the quilt to one end, then re-roll the quilt to the center and work toward the opposite end. To keep the sides of the quilt taut, you can run strips of twill tape around the stretchers and pin these to the lining with safety pins as shown in Figure 3.

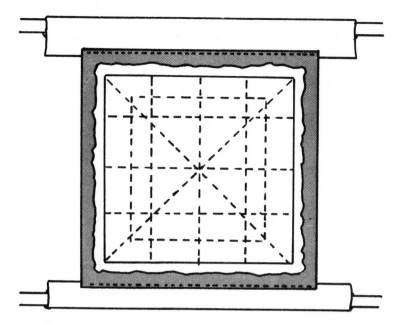

Figure 2. *After the layers are stacked, they should be pinned and basted with the stitches radiating from the center as well as lengthwise and crosswise. Here the piece is attached to the fabric strips of the quilting frame.*

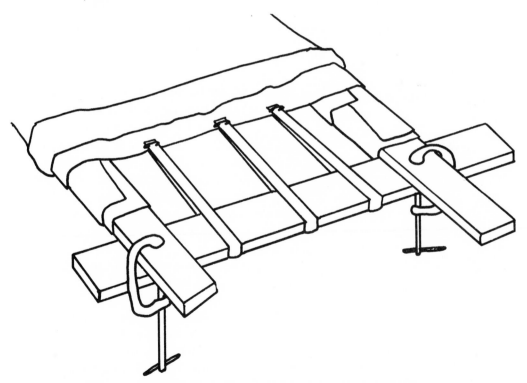

Figure 3. *After stacking and basting, the quilt is set into a simple frame made of stock lumber held together with C-clamps. Twill tape is wrapped around the end stretchers and pinned to the lining to keep the quilt taut.*

Machine Quilting

Machine quilting should not be regarded merely as a substitute for hand quilting; it has a unique quality all its own. There are those who believe that anything done by hand is better than something done on the machine. This standard may have had some validity years ago, but it certainly does not apply today. We can only speculate as to whether colonial women would have used machines if they had had them. It seems to me that unless there is an esthetic reason for doing a particular job by hand, there is no reason not to do it on the machine if that is faster and easier.

The machine can be used for joining pieces in patchwork, attaching linings and bindings, assembling garment parts, and any number of other tasks without sacrificing esthetic quality. The following will give some hints on how to use your machine for quilting.

The Presser Foot and Stitching. The pressure on the presser foot may have to be adjusted to accommodate thick padding, and a heavier needle may need to be inserted in the machine. The new ballpoint needles designed for knits are excellent for all fabrics. The length of the stitch will be dictated by the design, but generally it can be of medium length (6 to 10 stitches per inch) with the tension slightly looser than for normal sewing. You can use the automatic stitches that can be dialed on some machines, but they are rather mechanical-looking, except for the zigzag, which is excellent for appliqué.

The Darning Foot. Machine darning allows for greater maneuverability and freedom in stitching. In general, the technique involves deactivating the feed dogs, loosening the tension, and reducing the pressure on the presser foot. On some machines the darning stitch can be dialed, on others it is accomplished with the aid of a darning attachment. This is a darning foot that replaces the regular presser foot. It works on a spring, and therefore presses on the cloth only when the needle is actually in the cloth. When the needle is out of the cloth you can move the fabric freely and actually "draw" with the machine. The result is similar to a gesture drawing.

Some instructions claim that you can darn with the presser foot removed entirely, but I find that this causes the thread to knot and snarl. If possible, it is best to leave the presser foot on the machine and simply reduce the pressure until you can move the fabric freely with the presser foot lowered. In any case, the cloth should be held down with both hands so it is flat on each side of the needle. A hoop can also be used to keep the fabric taut. Machine darning is particularly effective when used as a decorative and textural accent with trapunto.

Tying and Tufting

Tying is an effective method of holding the layers of a quilt together when you do not wish to top-quilt. It does not take as much time as stitching, and it is especially good to use when the filler is too thick to sew through or when a woven filler has been used.

Thread a long, sharp yarn needle with a double strand of string, yarn, or crochet cotton. Insert the needle from the top through all the layers to the back, leaving about 2″ of yarn on the surface. Bring the needle back up to the surface about ¼″ away from where you started. Tie the yarn in a double knot and clip the ends to the desired length (see Figure 4). You can space the ties evenly or randomly according to the design of the top. If you do not want the tufts to show on the right side of the quilt, insert the needle from the back and tie on the wrong side. Then only a short stitch will be visible on the right side.

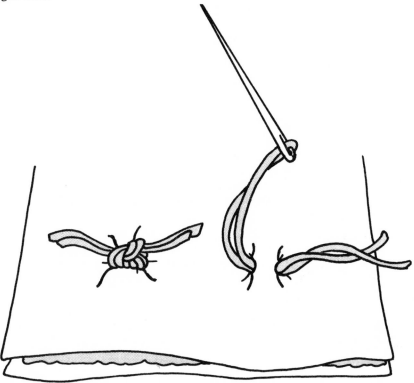

Figure 4. *For a tied quilt, a single stitch is taken with a double strand of yarn or string through all the layers and then tied in a double knot. The ends are then trimmed to the desired length.*

Joining Pre-Quilted Units

If space is at a premium, or if you prefer a more portable approach to quiltmaking, using the pre-quilted block is ideal. Determine the size of the block that you want—10″ to 14″ is good—and stay with that size for all the blocks. Treat each block as if it were a miniature quilt by preparing a top, filler, and backing all cut to the same size. The top of each block can be embellished by means of piecing, appliqué, painting, stitchery, or whatever technique appeals to you. The freedom of this approach allows you to combine several techniques in the same block, or a separate technique can be applied to each block. When stacking the layers of each block, make sure that the wrong side of the backing fabric is next to the filler. The backing

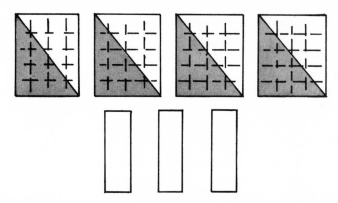

Figure 5. *For joining pre-quilted blocks, the squares are first arranged, then sewn together with vertical strips of fabric on both the front and back.*

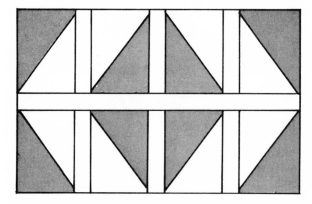

Figure 6. *Here the blocks have been arranged in a pleasing pattern, and have been joined with both vertical and horizontal strips of fabric.*

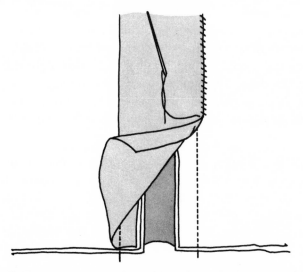

Figure 7. *Each front strip and one edge of each back strip can be joined to the block by machine. The remaining edge must be stitched down by hand.*

will also be the lining of the quilt, so you should take this into consideration when choosing the fabrics. You can make the quilt reversible by decorating both sides of the block. Each block is quilted either by hand or machine and set aside for later joining.

When all the blocks have been quilted, lay them out on the floor or table and keep shifting them around until you have a pleasing arrangement (see Figure 5). You can plan the arrangement of the blocks in advance for a more controlled approach. Join each block to the one next to it with strips of fabric (one on the front and one on the back) until you have a long horizontal row of blocks. The rows of blocks are then joined with long strips of fabric (Figure 6). As seen in Figure 7, the front strip and one edge of the back strip can be joined to the block by machine, but the remaining edge must be stitched down by hand.

Finishing

There are several methods of finishing quilted and patchwork items. The function of the piece will sometimes dictate how it will be finished; otherwise you can choose whichever method will best set off the piece.

Backing as Border. Trim the filler so it extends beyond the quilt top to the width of the desired border. The excess backing should be trimmed to twice the width of the desired border plus ½" for a hem. Press under the hem and then turn the backing over the filler to the front and pin in place. Sew down the border by hand or machine, taking care to miter the corners for a neat finish as shown in Figure 8.

Reversible Edge. Figure 9 shows how the top fabric and backing can be sewn together to give a finished look to both sides of the quilt. The top is trimmed evenly and folded over the batting. The backing is then folded under at the edge of the quilt and blind-stitched to the top along the fold.

Binding. Commercial bindings are available in a variety of colors, or you can make your own binding from the material used in the quilt. As shown in Figure 10, place the binding along the top quilt edge, right sides facing, and stitch ¼" from the edge. Turn the binding over the edge of the quilt to the back and blind-stitch in place. Wide borders and bindings can be given additional puffiness by laying in strips of batting before completing the final stitching.

Trimmings. Ruffles, fringes, piping, cording, or braid can be inserted between the quilt top and back for an additional decorative effect. For the bottom of a skirt, or another item that does not have a lining, the trim will have to be attached by means of a facing as seen in Figure 11. Lay the trim along the edge of the piece, right sides facing and raw edges together. On top of this, lay the binding or facing, right side down. Stitch, turn the facing to the wrong side, and hem into place.

Triangles. A beautiful sawtooth edge can be added to the bottom of a garment or the edge of a quilt by means of triangles (see Figure 12). Place two

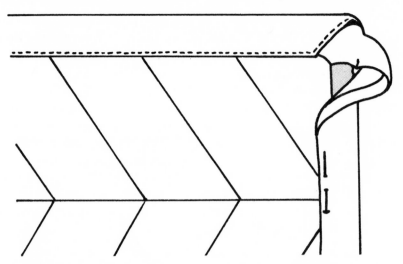

Figure 8. *If the quilt is to have a border, the backing fabric can be brought over the filler and top to make a neat edge with mitered corners.*

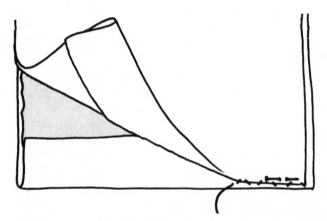

Figure 9. *For a reversible edge, the top is trimmed evenly and folded over the batting. The backing is then folded under at the edge of the quilt and blind-stitched to the top along the fold.*

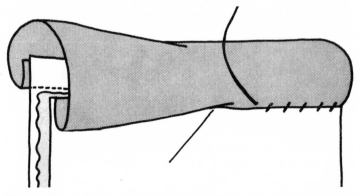

Figure 10. *To finish a quilt with bias binding, first trim all the layers evenly. Then sew the binding to the right side of the quilt and slip-stitch the other edge to the wrong side.*

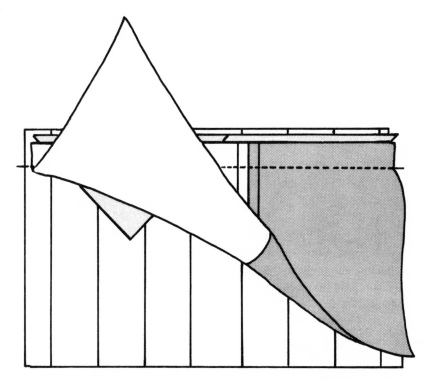

Figure 11. *Triangles or other trimmings can be inserted between the quilt top and backing, or attached with a facing as shown here.*

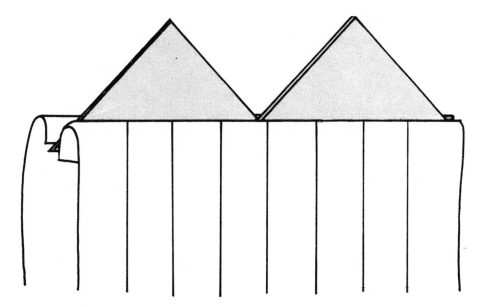

Figure 12. *Here the triangles have been turned to the right side for a zigzag edge.*

squares of fabric together, right sides facing, and stitch around all four sides. Cut the square diagonally from corner to corner, making two triangles. Turn each triangle to the right side and press. The triangles can either be inserted between the quilt top and backing, or attached with a facing as shown in Figure 11.

Lining

You may wish to finish your piece with a lining if you have not used a backing fabric before quilting. Cut a piece of fabric the same size as the top, and pin or baste it in place, right sides facing. Stitch along all the edges, leaving an opening large enough to turn the piece to the right side. After the piece is turned, close the opening with hand stitching. This technique can also apply to a piece that has not yet been quilted. In fact, you can insert the filler in the same operation by cutting a piece of batting the same size as the top and lining, then placing it on top of the lining material. You then stitch through all three layers, and your quilt is complete without the need for additional finishing.

Signing Your Work

Be sure to sign and date your work so future generations will know who made it and when. Your signature should be related to the quilt in such a way that it is not overly obtrusive, but still incorporated into the design. Whether you embroider by hand or machine will depend on which technique was used in making the quilt.

Patchwork

Scales by Michiko Sato, 70" x 102". A pieced quilt of strongly patterned fabrics based on a traditional kimono design. The quilt is lined but not top-stitched.

$\mathcal{P}$ATCHWORK IS A TERM that has been loosely applied through the years to both the technique of applying fabric to fabric (appliqué) and the joining together of many small bits of fabric (piecing). Today, patchwork has come to mean the same as "pieced work," and the two terms are used interchangeably.

Origins

As with appliqué, the early origins of patchwork and other fabric techniques have been lost in time. Few textiles, especially those subjected to hard use, have survived the ravages of time for more than a few generations, and quilting and patchwork are no exceptions. From the study of wall paintings and other art forms, historians have determined that the piecing of cloth shapes to form checkerboard and other geometric patterns was known in Egypt a thousand years before the birth of Christ. The piecing of silk and brocade was also known in ancient China, and it spread from there throughout Europe when the trade routes became established.

There are scattered references to patchwork in songs, poems, and household records early in the Middle Ages, and the most extensive use of the technique was for banners, tunics, and ecclesiastical vestments and hangings. While the earliest-known pieced quilt in England, consisting of chintz squares set together, is dated 1708, it seems unlikely that the technique was not known earlier. The practice of cutting individual motifs from scarce Indian chintz, and extending their use by appliquéing them to a cheaper ground fabric, influenced the development of patchwork as well. Eventually, in order to make every scrap count, the printed material was cut into smaller and smaller geometric shapes and pieced together with other fabrics to make quilt tops that more closely resembled the patchwork that we know today.

The Pieced Quilt in America. Although there are numerous examples of pieced English quilts of the eighteenth and nineteenth centuries, the pieced quilt in England never reached the artistic and technical heights that it did in America. It is not even known whether the craft developed independently in this country or was brought from England to the New World. The earliest known American pieced quilt occurs almost a century after the earliest English quilt, but somehow it does not seem possible that knowledge of the technique was lost for that period of time.

Whatever its origins, the patchwork quilt in America grew and developed out of necessity. Textile production was discouraged in the colonies in order to keep people dependent on English goods. Almost from the beginning there was a flourishing homespun industry, but it could not compete with the manufactured English cloth.

In the early years, the colonists were preoccupied with carving an existence out of the wilderness. Cash was scarce and making do was a way of life. Although some cloth did arrive from Europe on ships, it was expensive

Patchwork Quilt *by Romaire Bearden, 36" x 48". Collage of cloth and paper, and synthetic polymer paint on composition board. Worn fabric scraps are pasted on board to form the background for the stylized figure. The feeling of an actual quilt is beautifully conveyed. Collection of The Museum of Modern Art, New York, Blanchette Rockefeller Fund. Photo courtesy Cordier & Ekstrom, Inc.*

and hard to come by. Every scrap had to be saved, and clothes and bed-clothes were patched and repatched. The earliest quilts probably were of the "crazy" type, in which many irregularly shaped pieces were sewn together in a random pattern. This eventually led to trimming and cutting the patches into definite shapes of squares, rectangles, and triangles, giving rise to the first one-patch patterns. Still later, the geometric shapes were combined with each other to form patterns and then pieced in blocks.

In time a whole culture grew up around the quilting craft. For most rural women quilting offered not only a release from the harsh life, but an opportunity for self-expression. Little girls were taught to sew at an early age, and the baker's dozen of quilt tops was every young girl's goal by the time she was ready to marry. Quilting was woven into the social life of the women of the community. When a girl was betrothed she would invite her friends to a quilting bee to help make the bride's quilt. It was a time for gossip and socializing, and in the evening the menfolk would join the women for feasting and dancing.

In the early years of the colonies, style was dictated by what was fashionable in England. Chintz from India was as popular in America as it was in England, although design generally lagged years behind. From the time the colonies became a nation, designs were beginning to be adapted and simplified rather than slavishly copied. A unique American expression was developing, more straightforward and less pretentious than in England, and needlework was part of this renaissance. It is during this period, mainly the nineteenth century, that the most outstanding pieced quilts were created.

Hundreds of patchwork patterns were developed, named, and exchanged. The names of some of the patterns reflected symbolically what was socially or politically meaningful to the women at that time: *Jacob's Ladder*, *World Without End*, *Whig Rose*, *Star of Bethlehem*. Other patterns represented visual images: *Pineapple*, *School House*, *Wild Goose Chase*, *Bear's Paw*, *Log Cabin*. Patchwork patterns traveled west with the pioneers and changed names many times as the original name lost its meaning. For example, the design known on Long Island as *Duck's Foot in a Puddle* became *Bear's Paw* when it moved west. Although many favorite patterns were quilted over and over, the results were always different. The choices that had to be made along the way concerning pattern, color, fabric, quilting stitches, and borders reflected the individual preferences of the quilter, and no two quilts were ever alike.

Materials

Although any fabric can be attached to another, some fabrics are more suitable for piecing than others. Fabrics that are of medium weight, fairly firmly woven, and non-raveling are easiest to work with, especially for beginners. Heading the list for suitability would be most cottons or cotton and polyester blends, including muslin, gingham, calico, broadcloth, etc. If you are a beginner it makes sense to plan a simple project in an "easy" fabric to get the feel of the technique. Other factors to consider are the size of the pieces in the block and how the item will be used. Will it be washed frequently or will it be merely decorative? Will it be top-quilted or used as is? If the item is to be washed, you should select the fabric accordingly and pre-wash it before cutting. If the item is to be top-quilted, the fabric should be soft enough to allow the needle to penetrate all three layers without too much difficulty. Some silks are best left unquilted because the needle leaves a hole in the cloth, and on some wools the thread disappears into the nap, which makes top-stitching a waste of time. Traditionally, silk and wool quilts were tied rather than top-quilted, or they were used in a pattern calling for the direct application of the cloth pieces onto a muslin foundation.

In addition to cottons, other suitable patchwork fabrics are velvet, velveteen, corduroy, silk, satin, taffeta, wool, and double knits. Consider also the exotic possibilities of leather, suede, plastic or vinyl, and real or fake fur from worn coats and stoles. Combining fabric with fur in patchwork is an excellent way to recycle outdated fur garments, your own or thrift store finds.

Traditional Patchwork

Traditional patchwork patterns consist of geometrical shapes that are precisely sewn together to form a block. These blocks are then set together in a pre-planned way to make an overall pattern. I use the term "traditional patchwork" to define a method of working rather than the look of the finished product. Many contemporary artists are working with the geometrical shapes of traditional patchwork, but are not putting them together in the recognizable traditional patterns. For example, my quilted vest (page 105) was layed out and pieced in the traditional manner, yet the result is decidedly contemporary.

The simplest blocks are "one-patch," in which only one shape—such as a triangle, square, or hexagon—is used and repeated without using any other shape (Figure 13). Next in complexity is the four-patch block, which can be divided into four sections—two across and two down (Figure 14). The four-patch was probably the first true quilt block. Also common was the nine-patch block, consisting of nine equal units (Figures 15 and 16). From these relatively simple beginnings grew amazingly complex patterns. Once you have learned to dissect a block visually, you are on the way to designing your own patchwork.

Free Patchwork

Free patchwork is a more contemporary approach to piecing. It differs from traditional patchwork in that the pieces are not cut from templates, but are freely cut by eye and joined in a pleasing arrangement as shown in Figure 17. In colonial times this type of piecing was called "crazy," although it is not the same as the technique used in Victorian crazy quilts, where the fabric pieces were sewn down to a foundation fabric and embellished with embroidery.

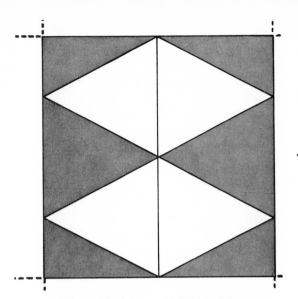

Figure 13. *A "one-patch" block has a design in which only one shape—such as a triangle, square, or hexagon—is repeated without using any other shape.*

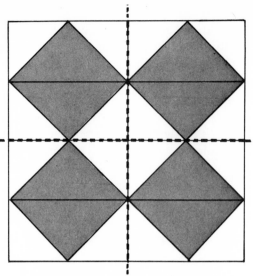

Figure 14. *The "four-patch" block has a design that can be divided into four equal sections as indicated here by the dotted lines.*

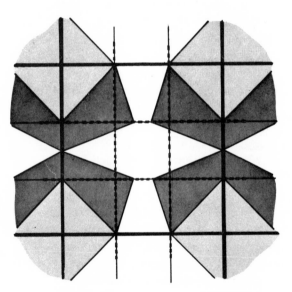

Figure 15. *As shown by the dotted lines, a "nine-patch" design can be divided into nine equal units.*

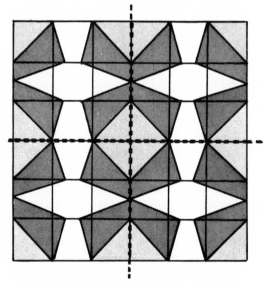

Figure 16. *Here four "nine-patch" blocks have been set together to form an all-over pattern.*

Figure 17. *In free patchwork, the pieces are randomly cut from the fabric and joined together in a pleasing pattern.*

Crazy Patchwork

Crazy patching is more closely related to appliqué than to piecing because it involves sewing down fabric scraps to a foundation rather than joining one piece to another. In the late 1800's, crazy quilts were made of elegant materials such as velvets, silks, brocades, and satins, and then elaborately embroidered along the seam line with cotton and silk floss. They were usually rather small and were used as throws and table covers rather than bed quilts.

To make a crazy quilt, cut a foundation square of muslin or some other inexpensive fabric. Starting in one corner, begin to lay in irregularly shaped scraps of fabric, overlapping them about ½" and turning under the edges. Baste the shapes to the foundation and then embroider, either by hand or with a machine zigzag stitch, along the seam lines.

Materials that are too heavy for conventional piecing—such as corduroy, wool, velvet, velour, etc.—are excellent for crazy patchwork.

Borders and Strips

A border on a quilt serves as a frame for the central motif. It should enhance and complement the overall design rather than compete with it. Usually the same colors and fabrics used in the quilt appear in the border, but not always. Some Amish quilts have extremely wide borders in which an entirely new color is introduced.

Figure 18. *Strips of pieced geometric shapes can be used as designs for entire quilts or as borders on quilts, hangings, or clothing. They can also be combined to piece an entire skirt or vest. These borders are from* Pattern and Design with Dynamic Symmetry *by Edward D. Edwards, Dover Publications.*

Borders can be made of strips of solid fabric, or they can be made of pieced geometric shapes as seen in Figure 18. Strips of pieced fabric can be used to make an entire quilt top, a dress, skirt, or vest, or even curtains or tablecloths.

Enlarging a Patchwork Block

You may want to enlarge a standard patchwork pattern for a single dramatic motif on a floor cushion, poncho, tablecloth, or bedspread. Fold a piece of paper that has been cut to the desired size into the same number of squares as are in the original block. With a ruler, draw in the diagonals to correspond to the original pattern. If you use heavy paper you can cut your templates right from the enlarged block and then proceed with marking and cutting the fabric.

Puff Patchwork

Sometimes called "biscuit" quilting, puff patchwork is a quick but creative method of making a luxuriously puffy quilt. The blocks can be set together randomly or according to a planned arrangement. Any patchwork design utilizing squares can be used as the basis for placement of the puffs.

The blocks can be any size desired, but 5" to 6" square is about right. After you determine the size and number of puffs needed for the design you have in mind, cut the proper number of foundation squares from muslin. Each muslin square should be ¼" larger than the desired size of each puff. Next, cut the same number of top squares, making them ½" larger all around than the muslin squares.

Make the puff by placing a top square on top of a muslin square, wrong sides together, and pinning them together at the corners. At the center of each top square, fold the excess fabric into a right-to-left pleat and pin the pleat to the muslin. Stitch around the three sides, ¼" from the edge, leaving the fourth side open for stuffing (Figure 19). Insert loose stuffing into the opening (Figure 20), taking care not to stuff too tightly. Make a pleat in the remaining side and stitch it closed. With right sides together, sew the puffs into rows, allowing a ¼" seam all around. Then join the rows and press the seams open. The quilt is now ready to be lined, and additional sheet batting can be inserted between the puff top and the lining for a heavier quilt. In any case, the finished quilt should be reverse-tied at intervals to keep the layers together.

Basic Patchwork Procedures

The following instructions will give the basic patchwork procedures that should be followed no matter how simple or complex your pattern might be.

Making Templates. A template is a pattern that is used as a guide in drawing and cutting patchwork pieces. A separate template is needed for each geometric shape in a block. You can buy templates made of plastic or metal, or you can make your own of cardboard, plastic, or sandpaper. Sandpaper grips

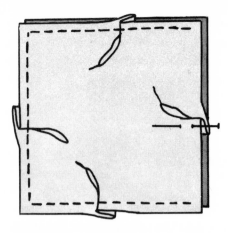

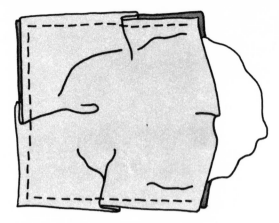

Figure 19. *For puff patchwork, two squares are placed together, wrong sides facing. The top square is a half inch or so larger than the bottom square, and a tuck is taken in the middle of each side. Three sides of the square are stitched down.*

Figure 20. *Here three sides of the square have been stitched, and stuffing is inserted through the opening. The remaining side is then stitched, and the puffs are joined together.*

the fabric for greater accuracy, but it wears out rather rapidly. Plastic makes a long-lasting template.

A successful patchwork project depends upon the accurate cutting and joining of each piece in the block. The cloth pieces will only be as exact as the patterns or templates from which they are cut. Therefore, it is well worth it to spend a little extra time on this important step.

After you have planned your block and drawn it to the correct size, trace each geometric shape onto tracing paper. Use a ruler or compass for absolute accuracy. Then, tape or pin the tracing paper to carbon paper. Place these, carbon side down, on the cardboard or plastic sheet. Again using a ruler or compass, draw around the geometric shapes, transferring the design to the cardboard or plastic. Cut out the templates with sharp scissors or a mat knife, taking care to be as accurate as possible. The template will be the same size as the finished piece, so a seam allowance will have to be added when the pattern is drawn on the fabric. The lines drawn on your fabric then serve as a seam guide. If you intend to stitch the pieces on the machine, you can include the seam allowance in the template and no allowance will have to be added when the fabric is cut. You do not need a drawn line for machine stitching because you can use the seam guide on the sole plate of your machine.

Laying Out Templates. Before laying out the pattern, press the fabric and draw out a thread for a straight edge. If the fabric length is not in alignment, you can generally "true" the cloth by gently stretching the fabric on the bias until it is squared. Squaring will enable you to lay out and cut the pieces with the greatest economy.

The grain of the fabric runs parallel to the selvage or woven edge of the cloth. If you are making a traditional pieced quilt, or an item that will not be top-quilted, you should lay out and cut the pieces in such a way that the finished product will not sag or pucker. The general rule is to place squares and rectangles with their edges parallel to the grain. Right-angle triangles should have one short side parallel to the grain, and isosceles triangles should have one side on the grain. Diamonds and parallelograms should have two parallel sides on the grain. Positioning the templates will be simplified if you mark the direction of the grain on them with an arrow. Always trim the selvage or exclude it in your layout as it will cause the pieces to pucker when sewn.

Marking and Cutting the Fabric. Place each template on the wrong side of the fabric, and draw around it with a pencil or chalk pencil as in Figure 21. If you have not included the seam allowance in the template you must add ¼″ all around each pattern piece for your cutting line (Figure 22). Be sure the pattern is lined up with the grain of the fabric as indicated on the template. Carefully cut out the pieces from the cloth along the outside drawn lines. Do not attempt to cut several pieces in layers as you will be unable to maintain perfect accuracy.

While there are few short cuts to cutting and piecing, if common sense dictates another approach, by all means try it. For example you can cut squares and rectangles by measuring instead of using a template as long as all the pieces come out the same size. If you are a beginner, or you are making a pattern for the first time, it makes sense to cut out the pieces necessary for one complete block and sew the block together to check for accuracy. Once you have cut out all the pieces for the whole project, it is difficult to make changes.

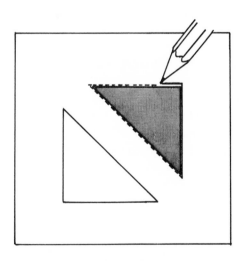

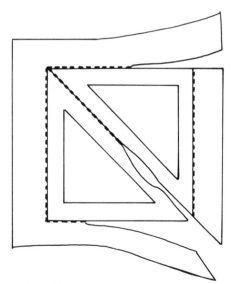

Figure 21. *The template is placed on the wrong side of the fabric and outlined with pencil. A ¼″ seam allowance should be added all around to determine the cutting lines.*

Figure 22. *After adding the ¼″ seam allowance, the pieces are carefully cut from the fabric.*

It is sometimes difficult for artists and craftsmen who have been used to working very freely with cloth to adapt to the rather tedious process of marking, measuring, and cutting hundreds of little pieces of cloth. Do not be put off, however; you will soon develop a rhythm for working that is soothing and pleasurable. Some people prefer to cut out the pieces for a project all at once and then begin sewing; others cut only enough pieces for a single block or a few blocks. You should always work in the way that suits you best. It should be fun, not torture.

Piecing the Block. Before beginning to sew, lay out the parts of a complete block to determine how it can be put together with a minimum of effort and with the greatest accuracy. Always work toward the longest seam possible. You will see that small triangles go together to form larger triangles, and triangles form squares that can then form strips. Starting from the center of the block usually helps the sequence fall into place. Once you have established the sequence for a block, continue with it for all the blocks of the same pattern.

Whether you are going to sew by hand or machine, place the patches together, right sides facing. Match the points and edges and pin. For machine stitching, insert the pins at right angles to the seam and stitch. Be sure to backstitch at the beginning and end of each seam to lock the stitching. For hand sewing, make an even running stitch along your penciled seam line. Using a fairly short needle will allow you to take several stitches at a time. For greatest possible strength, begin each seam by backstitching for three or four stitches. Do this at the end of each seam also and then knot securely. Naturally, the smaller your stitches, the stronger the seam will be. Hand-sewn seams should be pressed to the side for greater strength as well as to hide the seam. Machine-stitched seams can be pressed open or to the side, whichever you prefer. For accurate fit and to avoid puckering, press each seam before joining it to another section of the block. Use a single thread in a color that is similar to the fabric color, but not necessarily matching it.

While most patterns using simple triangles, squares, and rectangles can be successfully pieced on the machine, patterns with diamonds, curves, or more complicated geometric shapes are best done by hand—in fact these should be avoided entirely by beginners. Contemporary quilters, who are more interested in achieving exciting visual effects than showing off their technical skills, could spend a lifetime with the simplest geometric shapes and still not exhaust the possibilities.

Special Fabrics

The following will give you some hints on using special types of fabric in your patchwork designs.

Vinyls. Fabric-backed vinyls come in marvelous colors and patterns and are easy to sew on the machine. They make excellent bags, vests, skirts, belts, and rain ponchos, as well as floor cushions and furniture. Laying out and cutting is simplified because vinyls and plastics do not have a grain. Because of the thickness of the fabric, a ½″ seam allowance is better than the ¼″

usually allowed in piecing. Pins leave holes, so either pin into the seam allowance or use paperclips to hold the pieces together. Getting the seams to lie flat after sewing is sometimes a problem with these synthetics. If applying a warm iron on the wrong side fails, try taping with flexible plastic tape, top-stitching with the machine, or catch-stitching the seam to the fabric backing.

Furs. Pieced fur, either fake or real, can result in dramatic patchwork clothing. Small rugs, pillows, and hangings can also be made from fur scraps. The nap on fur usually runs downward, but subtle tone variations can be achieved by varying the direction of the nap. Lay out the pattern pieces on the wrong side of the fur and draw around them with a felt marker. Using a straightedge, cut out each piece with a razor blade, making sure to cut through the backing only. Before placing two patches together, smooth the pile away from the seam and pin into the seam allowance. If you have accidentally caught some of the pile in the seam you can gently lift it out with a blunt needle. To reduce bulk in the seam, trim away excess pile close to the backing. To make the seam lie flat, catch-stitch it by hand to the backing.

Knits. Knits have been extremely popular for home sewing in recent years, and it is more than likely that the scrap bag will yield several varieties. If a knit is not too sleazy or stretchy, it can be used for patchwork. Most double knits fall into this category. If you use a slight zigzag stitch for seaming, stretching will be minimal.

Finishing

Patchwork can be quilted or left as is and then finished according to the function of the item. There are, however, some special considerations concerning the finishing of pieced work.

Quilted Patchwork. The most common method of quilting patchwork is to follow the outline of each geometric shape by either stitching in the seam or just inside the seam line. For a less traditional look, the stitching can meander across the seam lines to form a pattern quite separate from the geometric shapes. Patchwork tops can also be tied as discussed in Chapter 2.

Unquilted Patchwork. In planning a project that will not be quilted, you must be especially careful about placing the templates correctly on the grain of the fabric. Otherwise the finished item will begin to sag and stretch after a period of time. It also helps to choose fabrics that are firmly woven and that are all about the same weight.

If the patchwork is for a wall hanging and is not to be top-quilted, it should be backed with a piece of non-woven interfacing and either top-stitched in the seam or tacked at intervals to prevent sagging. Hand or machine embroidery might also be used to provide stability as well as surface decoration.

Demonstration

A Crib Blanket

Step 1. *This demonstration is by Lynn Grimason. First a scale drawing is made of the design. The segments can be colored with markers to determine color placement. The next step is to make patterns for each shape in the design.*

Step 2 *(Below). Each geometric shape of the design is traced from the scale drawing and a ½″ seam allowance added. This much was allowed for the seam because of the weight of the material, a rather heavy no-wale corduroy. Each pattern piece is numbered and labeled for color before being laid out on the fabric (the arrows indicate the straight of the goods). Each piece is then carefully cut from the fabric.*

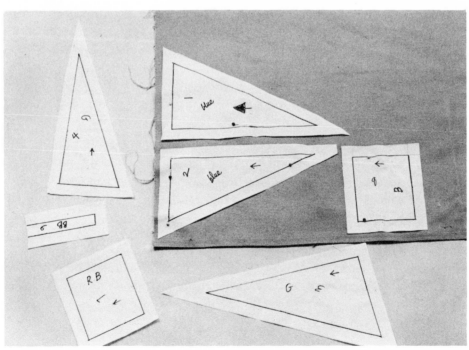

Step 3 *(Above). The pieces are joined by machine, first in sections and then in strips. The strips are then joined to each other according to the plan. The seams of each section are pressed open before the piece is joined to the next section.*

Step 4. *The surface is made in trapunto, and then joined to the pieced section. The moon, also trapunto, is placed into the pieced section by means of reverse appliqué; the star, a commercial embroidery patch, is sewn on by hand. A decorative border was added, then the piece was hand-quilted without a frame.*

Gallery

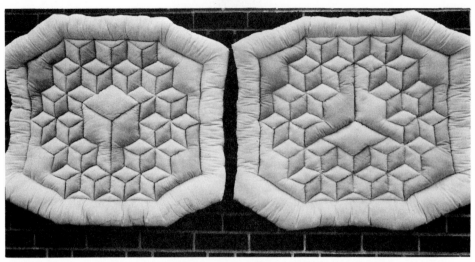

Dubious Information *by Joan Lintault, 31" x 73½". The traditional "baby block" pattern is given a new look in this two-part wall hanging made in cotton polyester. The patchwork is given an additional dimension by stuffing it from the back to raise the design from the background. Photo courtesy of the artist.*

Yellow Diamonds *by Michiko Sato, 68" x 89". The strong pattern in this quilt is developed entirely from squares and rectangles. Although pieced in the traditional manner, the quilt has a definite contemporary feeling.*

Odalisque VI *by Berni Gorski, 24" x 49". This raving beauty in a basket is crazy-patched of silks, satins, and velvets. It is further embellished with silk embroidery, beads, buttons, feathers, and has wrapped yarn for the hair. Photo courtesy of the artist.*

"George Washington Slept Here" *(Opposite Page) one of a series by Sante Graziani. Collage and acrylic on canvas. Fragments of actual patchwork are combined with painted areas in this contemporary work. Photo courtesy of the artist.*

Untitled Quilt *(Left) by Leigh Chadwick Eckmair, 80" x 80". Various fabrics, ranging in value from pale to dark, are skillfully set together to create the illusion of depth. Photo courtesy of the artist.*

Oriental Harbor Scene *(Below) by Peggy Moulton (detail). Small fabric scraps are pieced together and embellished with appliqué and decorative stitchery. Photo courtesy of the artist.*

Man's shirt, *Seminole Indian pieced work. Plain and pieced cloth strips of varying widths are joined horizontally to make this stunning shirt. Some of the strips are comprised of angled patchwork, a characteristic of Seminole work. Photo courtesy of the Museum of the American Indian, Heye Foundation, New York.*

Appliqué

Na Kalaunu Me Na Kahili (Crowns and Kahilis) *probably made by "Mother Rice," 75" x 75", Kauai, 1886. A beautiful example of a Hawaiian appliqué quilt done in red on white cotton. The fine quilting lines follow the pattern of the appliqué. Photo courtesy Honolulu Academy of Arts, Hawaii.*

*A*PPLIQUÉ IS THE PROCESS of attaching a cut-out fabric shape to a foundation fabric, usually by means of stitching. The term, from the French *appliquér*, meaning "to fasten to," also refers to the work created by this process or to the cut-out shape itself.

Origins

When woven fabrics became commonplace, man also saw the decorative possibilities of applying additional cloth shapes to the fabric surface. Perhaps appliqué was first discovered when it became necessary to patch a hole in a garment or bedcover. This may explain why the term "patchwork" has often been used through the years to describe appliqué or "laid-on" work as well as "pieced" work. The two techniques probably developed simultaneously in many parts of the world in conjunction with one another rather than as separate forms.

Appliqué, along with embroidery and other surface decorating techniques, was used extensively for church hangings and vestments throughout Europe during the Middle Ages. It apparently was not used in conjunction with domestic quilting until the sixteenth century, when the emerging middle class in England demanded more elaborate decoration in home furnishings and clothing. Great quantities of printed goods were being imported from India during that time, and this was to have a major influence on the development of pieced as well as appliqué quilts. Indian chintz was so superior to the European goods of the period that manufacturers in England and France pressed for legislation to curb its import. While their efforts were not entirely successful, it did slow the supply of chintz for a while, compelling women to make use of every scrap of imported cloth. The "palampores," or hangings that were previously used whole for bed hangings and covers, were now cut up and rearranged in the form of appliqué or pieced work. Individual motifs from the exotic "tree of life" designs were cut from the whole cloth, rearranged on plain white cotton or linen, and sewn down to make what were probably the first appliqué quilts. These spreads were elaborately quilted and often further decorated with fine embroidery in a technique called *broderie Perse*, or Persian embroidery.

Appliqué Quilts in America. Appliqué quilts enjoyed equal popularity with pieced quilts in the early years of the colonies, but were never commonplace due to the scarcity of whole cloth. The average family, struggling for its very existence in the New World, could ill afford the expensive goods being brought by ship from Europe. By the end of the seventeenth century, however, trade routes with Europe were firmly established and America began to develop her own textile industry, making yard goods more readily available to the homemaker.

Appliqué quilts, always considered special, were far more carefully crafted than pieced quilts of the time, and have survived to the present day in better

Broderie Perse Spread. *Appliqué of cut-out chintz, 106" x 107", eighteenth century. This immense spread illustrates the popular eighteenth and nineteenth century technique of cutting up expensive imported chintz and appliquéing the motifs to a white cotton ground. Photo courtesy of the Shelburne Museum, Inc., Vermont.*

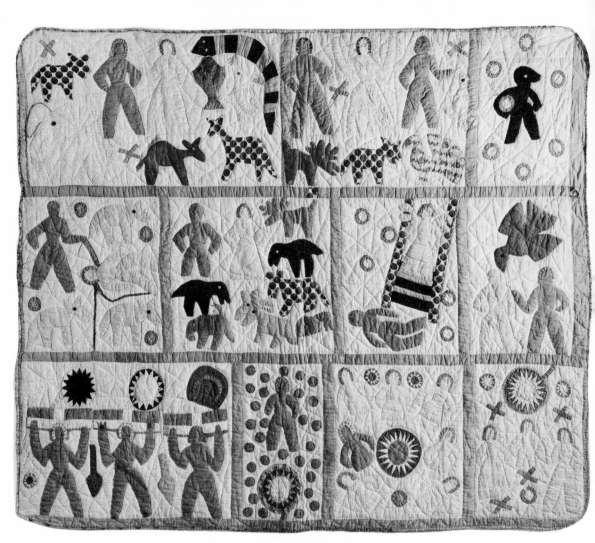

Bible Quilt *by Harriet Powers, Athens, Georgia, ca. 1886. Mrs. Powers was a negro farm woman whose deep feelings about her religion are expressed in these depictions of Bible stories. The appliqué shapes are turned under and stitched to the backing with the quilting done in rather random criss-crossing lines. Photo courtesy of the Smithsonian Institution, Washington, D.C.*

condition. Appliqué was most often the technique chosen for the bridal or "masterpiece" quilt on which were lavished the finest needlework and most expensive materials.

Released from the geometric rigidity of patchwork, appliqué provided the quiltmaker with the freedom to render in cloth the visions that danced in her head. Being pictorial rather than symbolic, the technique allowed for a more flowing, romantic expression than any other fabric form.

In addition to bridal and masterpiece quilts, there were album, presentation, and friendship quilts that were made by groups of women and perhaps presented to a respected member of the community, such as a minister who was leaving for another part of the country. The *Oregon Quilt* (endpaper) is an example of a contemporary presentation quilt that was made to call attention to the beauty and history of the state.

Hawaiian Quilting. The missionaries introduced quilting, patchwork, and appliqué to the islands in the 1830's. At first, having no scrap bags as did their New England counterparts, the Hawaiian women made quilts by cutting whole cloth into pieces and sewing them back together again. After a while this seemed unnecessary to them, and as whole cloth was available, they developed their own unique style of appliqué in which a single huge motif covered the entire quilt surface. The lush foliage of the islands inspired the intricate symmetrical designs that were cut from a whole piece of folded cloth. Some women became so skilled that they were able to cut the appliqué directly from the cloth, while others cut first in paper.

At first the quilting patterns were quite linear, but they gradually took on more flowing lines as the quilters began to follow the outlines of the appliqué. Quilts were put on frames just as in New England, but the supports for the frames were made in two sizes, high ones for the missionary ladies who used chairs and low ones for the Hawaiians who sat on the ground. In contrast to customs on the mainland, where quilt patterns were freely exchanged, Hawaiian quilters kept their patterns secret until the quilt was finished. Since quilt patterns were named by the designer and exchanged only by close friends, it was considered very bad manners to pirate someone else's design.

Materials

Almost any fabric is suitable for appliqué providing it is not too flimsy and does not fray excessively. Again, as with patchwork, some fabrics are easier to work with than others. The firmly woven cottons and cotton blends, such as percale, are generally the best. If the appliqué is to be turned under you should avoid any fabrics that are very loosely woven, slithery, or extremely bulky. Sturdy, washable fabrics should be used for items such as clothing that will be laundered a great deal. Felt is excellent for appliqué because the edges do not have to be turned under, but it does have to be dry-cleaned. Some synthetics, as well as silks, satins, wools, and velvets, should also be dry-cleaned but are excellent for use in hangings.

Designing For Appliqué

The complete freedom of expression afforded by the appliqué technique can sometimes inhibit the beginner. There are so many possibilities that it is hard to know where to begin. The women of colonial times drew ideas from the life around them, and that is a good place to begin. A design will be most successful if it is deeply meaningful to you. Nonrepresentational designs often arise out of a deep response to pure color or the rhythm of interacting lines and forms.

Appliqué can depict a scene or tell a story—such as a circus, a party, or flight to the moon. Some appliqué quilts are lushly padded velvets and velours reminiscent of country landscapes; others utilize the spontaneous collage technique of torn and cut fabrics embellished with stitchery and found objects. Any child would be thrilled to see his artwork adapted to appliqué and used in a quilt for his bed or the wall of his room.

The Appliqué Procedure

Whatever approach you choose, a good way to begin is by getting your ideas down on paper. Some people prefer to work spontaneously, by cutting the cloth directly without a guide, while others prefer to work from a planned design. Paper patterns can be cut for the larger shapes and the smaller details cut freehand and added later.

Making a Paper Pattern. First draw your design to scale on a piece of paper. Trace the various shapes from the scale drawing onto paper or cardboard to make a template. Lay the templates out on the right side of the fabric and draw around each shape with pencil, adding ¼″ all around if you plan to turn under the edge. If you wish, you can cut the shapes directly from the scale drawing and use those as patterns for cutting the fabric. The scale drawing can also be used as a guide for placing the shapes on the background material.

Preparing the Shape. If you do not plan to turn under the edges of the appliqués, you can begin to sew as soon as the shapes have been cut out. Otherwise you must clip both the outside and inside curves of the shapes to the pencil line as shown in Figure 21. To make small or intricate shapes easier to turn under, run a line of fine machine stitching (using matching thread) along the turn-under line before the shape is cut from the cloth. Then, cut out the shape on the outside line and clip the curves to the stitching.

You can press under the seam allowance before stitching, but it is best to pin the shape to the backing and turn under the allowance with your fingers as you sew. Pressing tends to flatten the shape, giving a rather mechanical look.

Sewing on the Appliqué. Each individual method of attaching the shape to the backing will affect the look of the finished piece. For a rounded look, especially if the appliqué is to be stuffed, it is best to turn under the edges and blind-stitch the shape to the backing (Figure 22). A raw edge that is

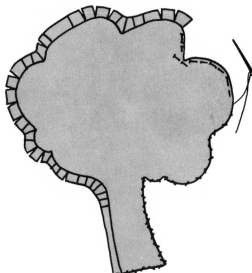

Figure 21. *After the fabric shape is cut out, clip the curves and corners to the turn-under line.*

Figure 22. *Turn under the seam allowance and pin it down. The edge is then blind-stitched to the backing.*

sewn down either by hand or machine tends to flatten the appliqué at the edge, but on the other hand allows for more surface decoration. Decorative embroidery stitches can be used with either a raw edge or a turned-under edge.

In traditional appliqué, the top of the quilt was appliquéd first, then the layers were stacked and basted, and the whole thing was put on a frame for quilting. The quilting usually echoed the appliqué shapes and the stitching was carried to the edge of the quilt. This method is especially noticeable in Hawaiian quilts where only two contrasting colors of cloth were used.

Machine Appliqué

Many contemporary quilters prefer to attach the appliqués and quilt in one operation, as was done with the *Voodoo Mask* on page 62. This can be done by hand, but can result in very sore fingers if the padding is thick. Sometimes it helps to use a curved upholstery needle instead of a straight needle.

For machine appliqué you can use either a straight or a zigzag stitch, but whichever you choose there are several approaches you can take. One is to stack the top and lining, right sides facing out, with the filler in between. Arrange the appliqué shapes on the top, and pin and baste through all three layers. Sew on the machine through all three layers, attaching the shapes and quilting at the same time. To avoid lumps and puckers, work from the center of the piece to the edges, smoothing out the fullness as you sew. If the padding is thick you may have to reduce the pressure on the presser foot slightly and perhaps lengthen the stitch a bit. When the entire quilt has been stitched you can finish the edges by binding them, or you can bring the backing over the top for a border.

Another approach is to place the top and lining together with the right sides facing and the filler in between. Seam around the edges through all three layers and leave an opening at the bottom for turning (as if you were making a pillowcase). Turn the piece to the right side and sew the opening closed by hand. Smooth out the wrinkles, and be sure that the seam is at the edge of the quilt. Next, arrange the appliqué shapes on the quilt top and pin. Baste through all the layers before sewing them down by machine. The advantage of this method is that when you have finished stitching, the quilt is automatically finished, needing nothing more in the way of lining or binding. The disadvantage is that as the stitching progresses, the batting can become unevenly distributed and cause lumps and puckers. This can be avoided somewhat by profusely basting all the layers together before beginning to quilt.

Stuffed Appliqué

A beautiful relief surface can be achieved by stuffing some or all of the appliqués in a quilt or hanging. Stuffed appliqué offers an opportunity for additional surface enrichment, and it can be combined with other techniques such as trapunto, stitchery, and patchwork. The appliqué is attached in the usual manner, either by hand or machine, but enough of an opening is left to insert loose stuffing before the final edge is sewn down (Figure 23).

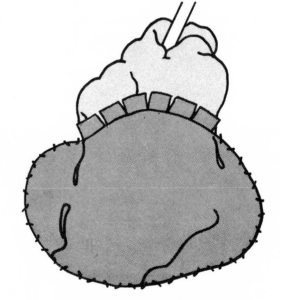

Figure 23. For stuffed appliqué, stitch the shape to the backing, but leave enough of an opening to insert loose stuffing before sewing down the final edge.

Reverse Appliqué

Reverse appliqué is the process of removing fabric shapes from the cloth to create the design rather than adding them. The technique is sometimes known as "cut-through" work, and it lends itself to extremely intricate designs.

Reverse appliqué is best known by the work of the Indian women of the Cuna region of Panama's San Blas Islands. Originally the work was done in rectangular panels that became the front and back of blouses called *molas*. These days the panels are made for export and are prized by collectors for use as hangings or cushion covers. The complicated designs, based on images encountered in daily life, often include copied lettering from discarded cans, boxes, or cigarette packages. Since the Indians do not read English, it does not bother them a bit to have the letters "Lucky Strike" parading across the front of a blouse; they only know that the shapes of the letters are visually pleasing.

Materials. A closely woven lightweight cotton, such as percale, works best because it does not ravel or fray. Heavy or slick materials would be difficult to work with as the amount of turn-under is much less than for conventional appliqué. Sharp, pointed embroidery scissors should be used to cut out very small shapes.

Cutting and Sewing. You should plan your design in advance so you will know how to stack the layers of cloth to get the effect that you want. Three to five pieces of cloth, all the same size, are stacked and basted together (see Figure 24). Draw the general outline of the design on the top layer, and using sharp, pointed scissors, cut through the top layer to the one beneath it. Clip the corners, turn the edges under and blind hem the edges of the top layer to the one underneath it with matching thread as shown in Figure 25. The turn-under will be about 1/8". Remember that the cut-out shape will become larger as the hem is turned under. The bottom layer of fabric is not cut, but serves as the background and lining.

The stitched layers of fabric result in a pleasant thickness that needs no padding and is ideal for clothing or a lightweight coverlet.

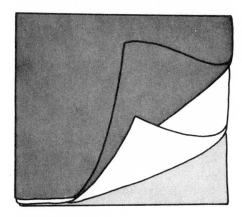

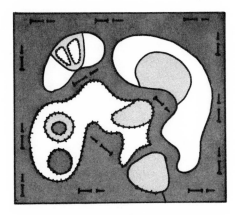

Figure 24. *In reverse appliqué, three or more pieces of different colored fabric of the same size are stacked on top of one another.*

Figure 25. *Shapes are cut away from each layer to expose the cloth underneath it. The bottom layer, in this case light gray, is not cut but serves as the background and lining.*

Demonstration   *A Voodoo Mask*

Step 1. *First a scale drawing is prepared and the colors filled in with felt markers. The design is traced onto another piece of paper, and the sections of the design are cut out to be used for patterns.*

Step 2. *The pattern pieces are pinned to the cloth and each section is cut out. No allowance is made for turn-under because the shapes will be sewn down by machine and the stitches will cover the raw edges.*

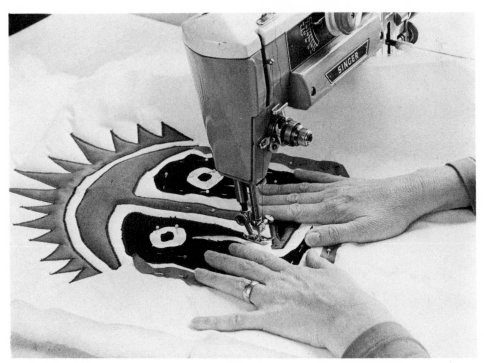

Step 3. *The backing, filler, and top are stacked with the fabric shapes placed on top. The shapes are then pinned down through all three layers. A zigzag stitch is used to appliqué the shapes and quilt in one operation.*

Step 4. *A piece for the back of the mask is cut and stitched to the front, right sides together. The seams are trimmed, and the mask is turned to the right side and hemmed. Notice how the lines of machine quilting accentuate the appliquéd forms.*

Gallery

Kenzo's Super Heroes by Michiko Sato, 70" x 84". Felt appliqué. For ease in handling, the blocks were appliquéd separately on the machine and then joined and lined. The quilt is used as a hanging in the bedroom of the artist's young son, who created the drawings that inspired the design.

Telephone Quilt *by Ann Marie Rucker, about 65″ x 85″. Felt appliqué. What at first glance appears to be an abstract design is really rows of digital telephones. This carefully planned appliqué is machine-stitched and quilted.*

Untitled *by Helen Bitar, about 50″ x 90″. Stuffed and flat appliqué in satin, velvet, cotton, polished cotton, and stitchery. The hand-stitched lines of the hair and features in this fantasy scene lend texture and contrast to the broad areas of appliqué.*

Trip Writer *by Kay Aronson, about 30″ x 45″. This piece is a collage-type appliqué of cut and torn shapes in various patterns and textures. It was both padded and quilted.*

Wedding Quilt *(detail) by Anne Kingsbury, about 4 x 5 feet. The unconventional use of leather, suede, and glazed ceramic beads lends an air of strangeness to this unique appliqué and pieced quilt. The hand-quilted cowhide oval with glued ceramic heads and appliquéd suede figures forms a central medallion surrounded by pieced leather and suede diamonds.*

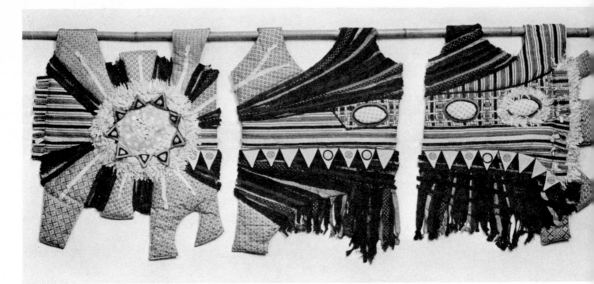

Welcome *by Peggy Moulton, about 35" x 72". A three-part banner in which the design is carried from one section to another to form a whole composition. Torn fabric strips are woven, fringed, and machine-appliquéd on padded forms.*

Landscape Quilt *by Gail Gosser, 42" x 78". The gently curving textured forms are turned under and stuffed. Feathers and three-dimensional conical forms are added to convey the feeling of landscape. Photo courtesy of the artist.*

Peaceable Kingdom *(Right) by Peggy Moulton, 30" x 50". A profusion of mythical critters are cut from various printed fabrics and machine-stitched to a padded muslin backing.*

Agnus Dei *by Patt Likos. A dreamy little world is created with satin, vinyl, and painted canvas appliqués. A feeling of space is achieved by stuffing the foreground shapes and flat-quilting the background. The lower area is fleece molded into sheep shapes.*

Trapunto

Bird of Prey *by Norma Minkowitz, 30" x 44". The rich texture of knitting and crochet is further accentuated by trapunto quilting on the wings and body of the bird. Notice the tiny female torsos at the bottom of the hanging. Collection of Mr. and Mrs. William Kokot.*

*B*ASICALLY, TRAPUNTO IS a form of quilting having areas of embossed design on a flat surface. It is made by outlining the pattern with stitching and then padding it with yarn or stuffing. In Italian, the literal translation, which means to punch or prick through, refers to the procedure of making an opening in the lining fabric through which the stuffing is inserted.

Cord-quilting (also known as Italian quilting) is closely related to trapunto. The main difference is that cord-quilting consists of roughly parallel lines of stitching that are stuffed by means of threading through them with yarn or cord. (In trapunto, the stuffed areas are the size and shape dictated by the design.) Traditionally, cord-quilted designs consisted of precise parallel lines of stitching that sometimes interlaced in elaborate curvilinear patterns. In contemporary work, the lines of the design may be roughly parallel, but precision and exactness are no longer considered that important.

In England and America, both trapunto and cord-quilting have, at different times in history, been referred to as "stuffed work." Today the term "trapunto" is generally used to describe both techniques, either corded or stuffed.

Origins

While the precise origins of trapunto and cord-quilting are lost in history, the fact that the earliest examples known came from Sicily probably popularized the term "Italian quilting." The absence of heavy inner padding, characteristic of quilting in northern climates, indicates that these quilts were meant to be purely decorative for use in a mild climate.

The earliest existing examples of trapunto, believed to have been completed toward the end of the fourteenth century, are three huge quilts that depict scenes from the life of Tristram. The similarity of workmanship and design in the three quilts suggests that they were probably the product of a common workshop. One of these quilts is in the possession of the Victoria and Albert Museum in London, and I was fortunate to have the opportunity to study it first-hand (see the photo on page 74). I was amazed at the enormous size (about 9 x 10 feet) and weight of the piece, suggesting that it would be more appropriate as a wall hanging rather than something to sleep under. The tiny, intricate figures and motifs are worked in a backstitch with heavy brown and natural linen thread on a canvaslike natural linen fabric.

This quilt inspired my early work in trapunto, although from the beginning I found it necessary to substitute machine stitching for hand stitching. Even by machine, the work is laborious and time-consuming, especially when the design is detailed and covers a large area of fabric.

Stuffed Work in England. Although bed quilts, cushion covers, and other household items were cord-quilted, the technique reached its height of creativity and craftsmanship in the eighteenth century, when it was used to

Dress Detail, *English, mid-eighteenth century. This motif was cord-quilted on linen with a running stitch. Courtesy of the Victoria and Albert Museum, London.*

Linen Coverlet, *Sicilian, about 1400. Trapunto-quilted in brown linen thread on natural linen, this piece shows scenes from the life of Tristam. Courtesy of the Victoria and Albert Museum, London.*

American "White Work" *(Right), about 1840. This detail shows fine hand stitching on white cotton fabric. Collection of the author.*

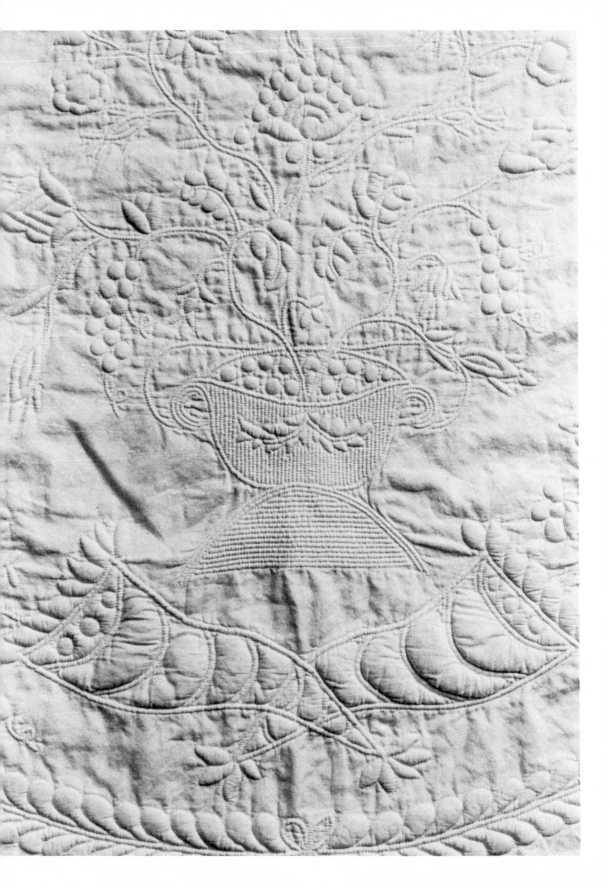

decorate clothing. Jackets, waistcoats, and caps for men, women, and children were elaborately cord-quilted and often further embellished with embroidery in the unstuffed areas. The considerable skill and time required to execute this delicate work suggests that it was done by servants for the wealthy rather than as a cottage craft. Also, the fine cotton, linen, and silk fabrics and threads were expensive and hard to come by, well out of the reach of peasants.

By the end of the eighteenth century, cord-quilting gave way to padded quilting, although it has occasionally reappeared on small pieces in the twentieth century.

Stuffed Work in America. From England, stuffed quilting spread to the colonies and was extremely popular from 1820 to 1850. However, the scarcity of cotton and the fine stitching required made the technique rather rare. Most of the work came from the south or the cities where ladies had the required amount of leisure time. In America, stuffed work was called "white work" because it was always worked on fine white cotton fabric. The extremely fine stitching required was considered the ultimate test of craftsmanship, so no woman would attempt it until she had complete confidence in her needlework skills.

Trapunto Today

Traditionally, trapunto was almost always worked on plain fabric, usually white or cream-colored. The idea was to create a relief surface, dependent for its life on the effects of light and shadow alone. Today, contemporary artists are using this ancient technique in ways that its discoverers never visualized. While many of the new relief forms have been influenced by traditional techniques, in all probability the artist is often not even aware that what he is doing is quilting. Trapunto is being used with great imagination by contemporary artists to pad out surfaces that have been previously painted, dyed, printed, stitched, or otherwise embellished. It is even being used to give additional dimension to hand-knitted and crocheted surfaces in conjunction with three-dimensional forms.

Materials and Tools

Of all the quilting techniques, trapunto allows you the most freedom in your choice of fabrics. Any material that can be sewn is suitable.

For the top, almost any fabric may be used, from heavy canvas to a sheer nylon stocking. Fabrics with a nap, such as velvet, corduroy, velour, and suede cloth provide a luxurious, soft relief surface. Lightweight and sheer fabrics tend to pucker and will give a more agitated surface. Cotton and cotton blends produce sharply outlined forms. Linen, silk, satin, synthetics, knits, and all kinds of curtain and drapery fabrics can also be used. A fabric that has some body is the best choice for a beginner as sheer fabrics are more difficult to handle, especially with machine sewing.

For the backing, choose a loosely woven, lightweight fabric such as voile, scrim, organdy, or lightweight muslin. If the backing is semitransparent it will enable you to see how the stuffing is being distributed in the shape without constantly turning the work to the right side. For stuffing, loose polyester fiber is now readily available and is more satisfactory than cotton. Some bulky yarn is needed for cord-quilting. This is becoming hard to find, but is sometimes sold in small amounts for the purpose of tying pony tails or gift packages. Thick wool yarn or rug yarn can also be used. Mercerized cotton sewing thread is best for both hand or machine sewing, as synthetic threads tend to knot and fray.

You will need a large-eyed, blunt yarn needle for cord-quilting. Smaller blunt needles, called tapestry needles, are good for stuffing very tiny shapes. For trapunto, you should have a knitting needle (or some other suitable instrument) for poking the stuffing into small areas. I find that a small knitting needle or crochet hook with a bit of masking tape wrapped around the pointed end for traction is most useful for pushing in the stuffing. Small embroidery scissors with sharp points are easier to use for cutting slits in trapunto than large shears that might slip and damage the fabric.

Trapunto Techniques

The techniques for trapunto are simple and can adapt to a wide range of designs. The first thing to do is to plan your design on paper, then transfer it to the wrong side of the lining fabric. The best method for transferring is to use a tracing wheel or a blunt needle and dressmaker's carbon paper. When planning your design, remember that the image you draw on the back of the fabric will be a mirror image of what will appear on the top layer of fabric. You can also draw directly on the lining fabric with chalk if you have your design well in mind before you start.

Lining. Pin the lining fabric to the wrong side of the fabric to be quilted. If the design is to be a small spot of trapunto — as on the front of a dress — the lining needs to be a piece only a couple of inches larger than the outer edge of the design area. However, if the entire area is to be heavily stitched and padded — as in a quilt or a wall hanging — the lining should be the same size as the top piece of fabric. It should be held firmly in place with basting stitches that radiate from the center of the fabric to the edges.

Stitching. As in most quilting procedures, it is best to begin stitching in the center of the fabric whenever possible and then work out to the edges. If a previously prepared design is to be used, it should be transferred as described earlier and the stitching should be done from the wrong side. For a more spontaneous effect, the stitching can be done from the right side so you can see the design emerge as you work.

Either way, a simple running stitch is used to define the outline of the shapes. A single thread is sufficient unless you particularly want to accentuate the stitching, in which case you could use a double thread. Care should be taken *not* to pull the stitches too tightly or the fabric will pucker. After stuffing, there is a good deal of puckering anyway, and you don't want to add to this from the start.

Stuffing. When all the stitching has been completed, remove the basting and turn your piece to the wrong side. With sharp embroidery scissors, make a small slit in the lining fabric only, in the center of each area to be padded (see Figure 26). The size of the slit is determined by the size of the area to be stuffed. It is best to make a cut just large enough to allow you to insert the stuffing without a struggle.

Stuff each area, using your knitting needle or stick to poke small amounts of stuffing through the slits. Check the front occasionally to make sure the stuffing is evenly distributed. If the stuffing is very tightly packed, there will be a good deal of puckering and drawing up on the right side, and the surface will be rather hard. Unless you want this effect, you must take care not to stuff too tightly. When the stuffing has been completed, close up the slits with a whipping stitch (see Figure 27). If the fabric is fairly heavy, iron-on tape can be applied over the slits to save you the trouble of sewing them. You should experiment with this in an unobtrusive spot, however, as the pressure of the iron may flatten the right side and may also cause an unpleasant stiffness if soft fabrics have been used.

Cord-Quilting

The technique of cord-quilting can be used for a whole design or for accent areas within a trapunto design. In either case, the design is composed of roughly parallel sewn lines, which are then stuffed with yarn or cord. Lining and stitching follow the same basic procedures as trapunto.

To stuff the lines of stitching, thread a large-eyed, blunt yarn needle with bulky yarn, poke it through the lining fabric, and run the needle between the layers of fabric and between the parallel lines of stitching as shown in Figure 28. After a few inches, poke the needle through the lining fabric again to the surface. Draw up the thread and reinsert the needle through the exit hole. Then draw through for another few inches (see Figure 29).

This technique is also quite useful for details in trapunto designs that are too small to slit and stuff.

Trapunto on a Sewing Machine

Although hand stitching is suitable for small pieces and is very beautiful and satisfying to do, many contemporary quilters prefer to use the sewing machine for trapunto. The stitching itself may be the only design, or it can follow previously painted, printed, batiked, or screened designs. When using a regular stitch, you will have to turn the piece carefully in the machine so the stitching follows the lines of the design.

Where greater freedom and maneuverability are desired, a machine that provides for darning is a great help. This technique is explained in detail in Chapter 2 under "Machine Quilting."

In my own work, I rely very heavily on the darning foot to fill in areas of the unstuffed background with solid masses of stitching. This not only allows for the addition of texture, but for subtle tonal variations as well when different colored threads are juxtaposed.

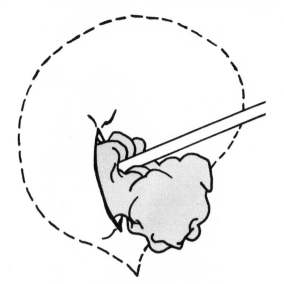

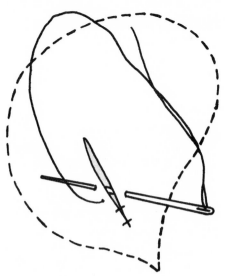

Figure 26. *Baste the lining to the wrong side of the fabric to be quilted. Stitch the outline of the design by hand or machine through both layers. Cut a slit through the backing only in the center of each outlined shape; with a stick or knitting needle, poke small amounts of stuffing through the slit, padding out the shape.*

Figure 27. *Take care not to overstuff, but just uniformly raise the design from the surface. After stuffing, close the slit with a whipping stitch.*

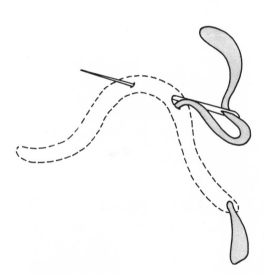

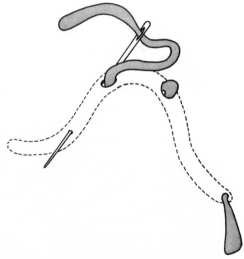

Figure 28. *Baste the lining to the wrong side as for trapunto, and stitch a design of parallel lines by hand or machine through both layers of fabric. Thread a blunt needle with bulky knitting yarn. Insert the needle by poking a hole through the lining, and bring the yarn between the layers of fabric and inside the two lines of stitching. Run the yarn along for several inches before bringing it to the surface.*

Figure 29. *Bring the needle and yarn to the surface. Draw the yarn through, then reinsert the needle through the exit hole, following the lines of the design. A small loop should be left at each exit point to prevent puckering. Repeat this procedure throughout the design. The entering and exiting "tails" of yarn should be trimmed to about ½".*

Demonstration

A Face Pillow

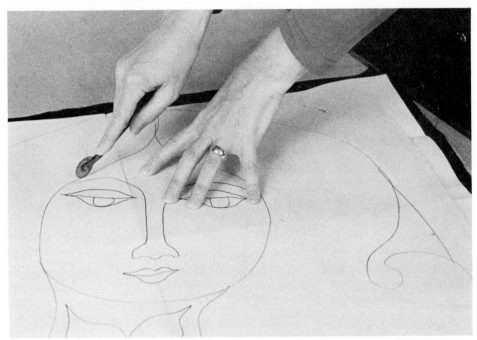

Step 1. *Using dressmakers' carbon and a tracing wheel, trace the design onto the lining material.*

Step 2. *The layers are basted together with stitches radiating from the center. With a darning foot (a regular stitch can also be used), the lines of the design are traced with the sewing machine. Since the bobbin thread will show on the right side, it is important to wind the bobbin with the proper color, in this case an off-white.*

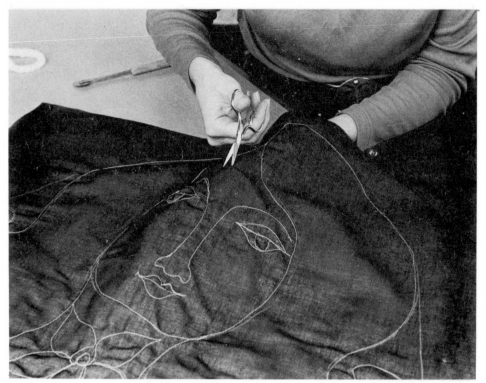

Step 3. *Sharp, pointed embroidery scissors are used to slit the lining fabric in each of the areas defined by stitching.*

Step 4. *Small amounts of polyester stuffing are poked in between the two layers.*

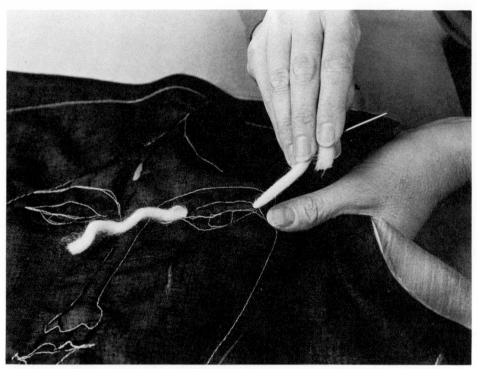

Step 5. *For small or narrow areas, such as eyebrows and lips, a blunt needle threaded with bulky yarn is inserted and drawn through.*

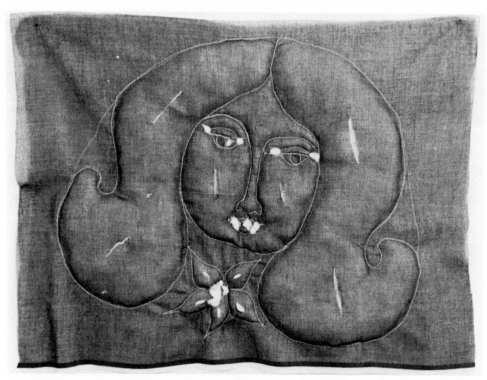

Step 6. *The entire design is padded. The slits can be closed with a whipping stitch or iron-on tape.*

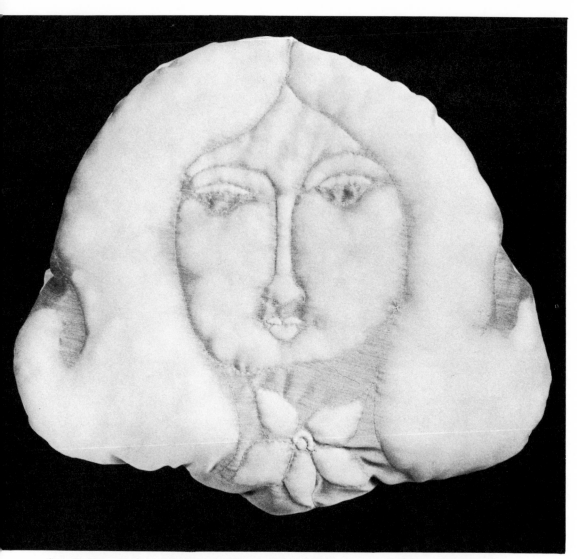

Step 7. *The pillow is finished by cutting a piece of fabric for the backing and placing it on the quilted pillow front, right sides together. All the layers are then stitched together around the outer perimeter of the design, leaving an opening at the bottom for turning. The seams are trimmed to ½" and the pillow is turned to the right side. Stuffing is inserted and the bottom opening closed with a blind-stitch.*

Gallery

Lily of the Flower *by Joan Blumenbaum, 21½" x 25½". The sensuously padded trapunto beautifully sets off the delicate hand stitchery of the central figures. Photo courtesy of the artist.*

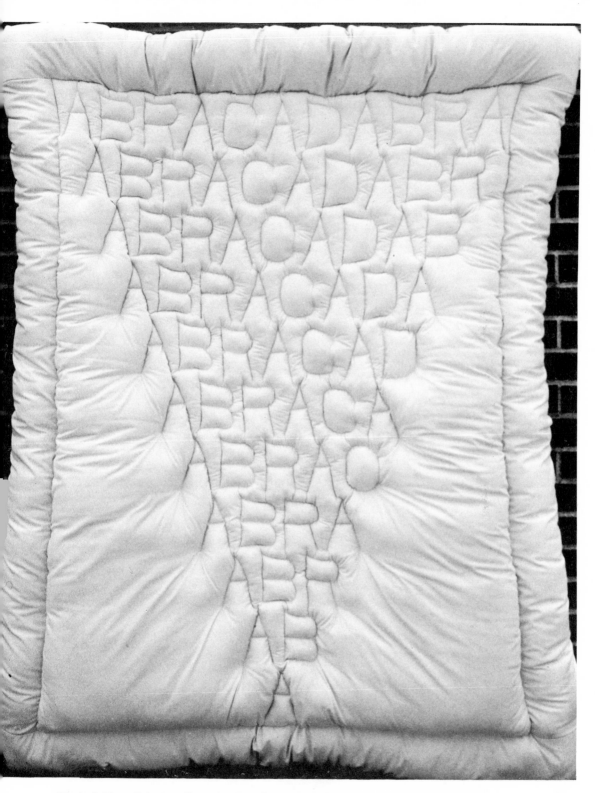

Magical Chant I Against Fever *by Joan Lintault. Polyester-cotton fabric is machine-stitched and stuffed in this unique hanging that coveys a sense of visual magic. Photo courtesy of the artist.*

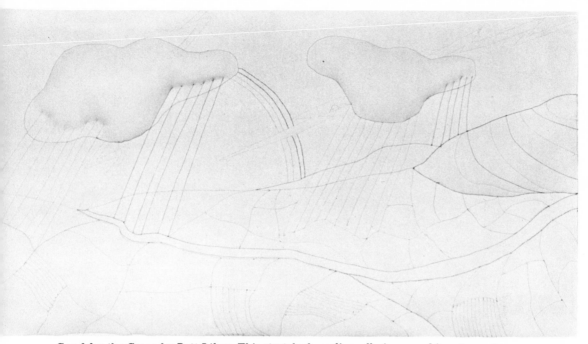

Good for the Crops *by Patt Likos. This stretched muslin wall piece combines trapunto with regular quilting. The stitching is done by hand with various colored threads.*

Girls and Birds *(Left) by Elsa Brown, 50"
x 84". A trapunto quilt in off-white
dacron is used as a wall hanging in a bedroom. Collection of Julie Schafler.*

Figure Studies *by Elsa Brown, each 12" x 6". Scraps of nylon stockings have been used for these machine-stitched trapunto figures.*

Untitled (Right) by Kathryn McCardle Lipke, 58" x 40". Quilted and stuffed natural linen gauze is combined with loosely-knotted natural jute rope. Photo courtesy of the artist.

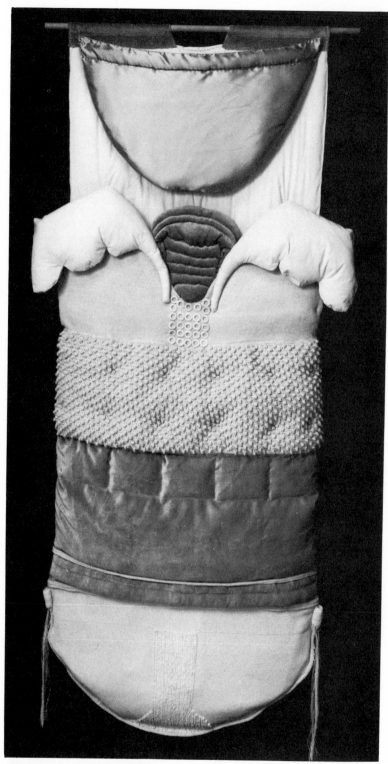

Wall Hanging/Sleeping Bag *by Norma Minkowitz, 33" x 80". Muslin, cotton, satin, velvet, and dacron. Knitting and crochet provide the texture for this sensuous sleeping bag that is given further dimension with trapunto stuffing.*

Clothing

Panamanian Mola. *The front and back of this blouse, called a mola, is made of two colorful reverse appliqué panels. The intricate work is done by the Cuña Indians of the San Blas Islands off the coast of Panama. Collection of Norma Minkowitz.*

*Q*UILTING AND patchwork have long been used for clothing in many parts of the world. The obvious insulating properties of layered cloth against both cold and heat were discovered by man centuries ago, and this principle is still in use today. In northern countries, garments are quilted with thick wool interlinings to keep out the cold; in desert regions, outer garments made of lightly padded and corded cotton or silk keep out the intense heat. The resourceful Chinese invented dual-duty garments made of cotton with inner pockets provided for inserting padding when the weather turned cold.

Origins

In Europe, quilted and padded armor was widely used during the early Middle Ages. A fairly consistent picture of its use can be built from records, household inventories, and the works of poets and song writers. Quilted armor of heavy linen or canvas provided reasonably adequate protection against the sword, spear, and arrow, but fell into disuse when the weapons of war became more sophisticated. As chain mail and plated armor came into use, the quilted garment was worn underneath to protect the body from chafing and bruising. Considering the wear and tear that these garments underwent, it is no wonder that only a few fragments have survived to the present day. According to records, domestic quilting of the eleventh through thirteenth centuries did not enjoy the same importance as quilted armor of the period. But as certain types of armor could be made at home—such as the habergeon (a sleeveless, quilted jacket) and the jack (a sleeved coat)—it seems likely that these techniques were applied to domestic body coverings as protection from the elements.

Quilting was not used extensively on clothing until the seventeenth and eighteenth centuries in England, and then it was not for outer wear. Cord-quilting became a craze on men's and women's garments toward the end of the seventeenth century and remained so for nearly a hundred years. The extremely fine work was done on white cotton or linen and sometimes additionally embellished with open work or embroidery. Cord-quilted caps made in sections were popular for both day and nighttime wear to ward off drafts.

In cold climates, petticoats were quilted for warmth as well as for show. Elaborate quilting on silk and satin was done in the urban areas, and simpler quilting on rough wool and linen was done in the country. Corsets and other undergarments were elaborately cord-quilted to give support to the cotton fabrics.

Contemporary Applications

Today, in spite of heated homes and cars, quilted fabrics continue to be used for garments where warmth is a requirement: ski jackets, coats, robes, vests,

Olive Green Doublet *of quilted silk, French, about 1635. Courtesty of the Germanisches Museum, Nuremberg.*

Patchwork Dressing Gown, *English, late nineteenth century.*
This man's dressing gown was made from pieced silk hexagons.
Courtesy of the Victoria and Albert Museum, London.

Dress, *made by the Seminole Indians of Florida, is constructed of plain and pieced strips set together. The varying widths of the strips are beautifully proportioned. Photo courtesy of the Museum of the American Indian, Heye Foundation, New York.*

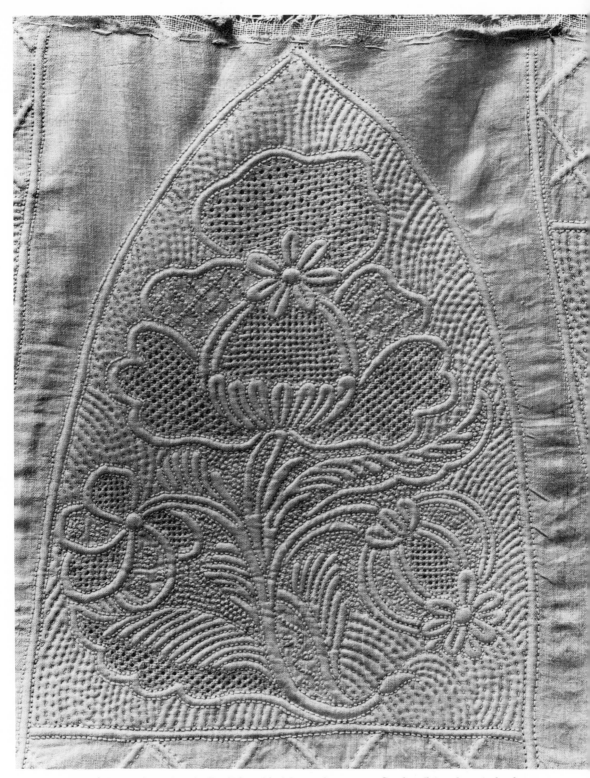

Man's Linen Cap *(detail), English, mid-eighteenth century. Cord-quilting done in back and running stitches, drawn work, and French knots decorate this fine linen piece. Courtesy of the Victoria and Albert Museum, London.*

sleeping bags, snow suits, etc. Practical considerations aside, both quilting and patchwork offer limitless possibilities for self-expression by contemporary artists and craftsmen. The use of the term "body coverings" instead of "clothing" conveys the shift in thinking from the restrictive and conventional toward freedom and individuality.

Padding and quilting can add dimension to the body where it is wanted, and at the same time it can camouflage hills and valleys that are considered too obtrusive. Piecing is a perfect technique for using scraps and remnants that would otherwise end up in the wastebasket. It allows you to make use of a remnant or scrap in a favorite color or texture that is too small for a whole garment.

Recycling

In the current spirit of recycling, the good parts of a worn patchwork quilt can be recut and given new life as a one-of-a-kind garment. Most antique quilts are rather thin and therefore suitable for skirts, vests, capes, ponchos, or coats. Occasionally, in antique shops, you can find unquilted tops or blocks that have been pieced but not set together. They can be incorporated into clothing as borders around the bottom of a skirt, sleeve, or pants. They could also form panels down the front or back of a dress or tunic.

I would hesitate to cut into a really lovely unquilted top as it would seem almost sacrilegious. If the top is large enough, however, you could consider using the whole piece as a caftan, in which case you would have to make only a small opening for your head. Parts of an old fur coat can be cut into sections and joined with pieces of plain fabric or leather to create an entirely new garment.

Quilting With a Pattern

You can make a quilted or patchwork garment by quilting yardage in an overall design and then making up the garment in the usual way. The patchwork shirt on page 106 was constructed this way and it is very effective visually. If you prefer to have more control over the outcome, however, you will find it challenging to tailor the quilting or patchwork to the shape of a specific garment. Non-fitting garments, such as ponchos, capes, and gathered skirts, can be constructed without careful fitting or even a pattern. Coats, vests, tailored skirts, and the like usually require a pattern and must be carefully constructed so they will fit properly.

Selecting a Pattern. In selecting a pattern for a quilted or patchwork garment, avoid fussy details such as gathers, tucks, pleats, etc. Patterns specifically designed for leather garments do not have darts or tucks and are therefore easily adaptable to quilting. Bear in mind that quilted fabric, like leather, has very little "give." Also, because of the bulk, it can result in a tighter fit than a single layer of fabric. You will find that you may have to add an inch or two to the seams of a favorite skirt pattern or you may not be able to sit down in it.

Tailoring a Garment

The following instructions will describe how to make a patchwork garment that is also quilted. The same procedure applies to making any quilted garment, regardless of the technique used for decorating the top layer. In any case, the top or outer layer of the garment is prepared first by painting, printing, appliqué, piecing or whatever. It is usually best to draw the outline of the pattern section on the cloth with pencil or chalk, cut out the shape roughly, and apply the decoration before cutting the piece out along the pattern lines.

Laying Out the Pattern. Lay out the pattern pieces on the backing (lining) fabric and draw around each piece with chalk or a soft lead pencil. Since the fabric is not folded but opened out flat, you will have to flip over any pattern piece that would ordinarily be placed on the fold so you have a diagram of the whole garment section.

With a yardstick, draw a line corresponding to the straight of the goods. Using this line as a guide, draw a grid of 3″ squares right on the cloth within the outline of the pattern. This will serve as a guide for keeping the patchwork straight. Now, roughly cut out the drawn garment sections so they will be easier to handle.

Piecing. Assemble the fabrics that you intend to use and begin cutting out the patchwork pieces. You can cut and lay out all the pieces before sewing, or you can seam sections together as soon as you have a pleasing arrangement. The latter method seems preferable so you can get an idea of scale. When all the pieces are joined, turn the section to the wrong side and press.

Quilting. Assemble the layers as if making a quilt. The piece of lining fabric with the pattern drawn on it will go on the bottom, with the drawn lines next to the filler. Leave some extra filler and lining showing around the edge. Pin the layers together a few inches out from where you will begin to quilt. The easiest type of quilting is to use a simple running stitch just inside the seam line of each geometric shape, but you can use any quilting pattern that you wish. As the quilting progresses, the fullness is smoothed out to the edges and the pins reinserted in the unquilted areas. You can baste the layers together rather than pinning, but in either case, check the back frequently to make sure that no wrinkles have developed in the backing. Bring the stitching just to the seam line—do not quilt the raw edges as they will be incorporated in the seam allowance.

Cutting Out the Pattern. Re-lay the pattern, pin it down, and cut along the edge through all the layers. If there is a dart in the pattern, pin it together in the tissue piece and align it with the corresponding dart in the pieced top. If the design contains elements such as blocks or strips that must be matched at the seams or in front, be sure to mark them on the pattern before the final cutting. Pin the pattern firmly through all the layers and cut out the garment section.

Darts. The best time to sew in the dart is usually in the pieced outer layer before the layers are assembled. A dart can be made right in the patchwork, but it should be cut along the fold and pressed open after sewing. When a surface decorating method is used, such as appliqué, stitching, or painting, it would seem best to put in the dart in the fabric first so as not to spoil the design. In trapunto, the dart should be put in before stitching and stuffing.

Finishing. When all the sections of the garment have been pieced and quilted, assemble the garment in the usual way and finish by lining or binding the edges. Before lining, you can pluck the batting out of the seams to reduce the bulk, and press the seams open.

Backing as Lining. When the backing also serves as the garment lining, you will have to put the darts in the lining as well as the top, and then align them when the layers are put together. Remember to bury the knots in the filler and end with a back stitch. If the garment is assembled in the usual way, you can hand sew wide bias tape over the seam to hide it as shown in Figure 30.

Making Clothing from Blocks and Strips

Vests, skirts, dresses, even pants and shirts can be made by joining plain and pieced strips of fabric. An entire garment can be constructed this way, or a strip of patchwork can be used for a border around the bottom of a skirt or pants to add weight and decoration. The Seminole Indians of Florida used this method extensively to make skirts, dresses, shirts, and capes. In the dress on page 95, the widths of the pieced and plain strips have been set together in varying proportions. The result appears intricate, but in reality the technique is quite simple. The pieced skirt in the gallery is a contemporary adaptation of this technique. The strips are easily pieced on the sewing machine, and only straight sewing is required to set them together.

A skirt or vest can also be made of blocks that have been appliquéd or otherwise decorated and then sewn together. If the garment is very flaired at the bottom, the blocks will have to be tapered so they are parallel to the hemline. For this reason, it is usually best to choose a pattern that does not have a great deal of flair.

Piecing the Whole Garment

A unique patchwork garment can be made by seeing the whole garment as an irregularly shaped block (Figure 31). Draw each pattern piece to scale on a piece of wrapping paper. Where the pattern indicates that the piece is to be placed on the fold, simply draw around one side, flip it over, and draw around the other side. With a ruler or yardstick, draw a geometric design on the wrapping paper pattern. If the design is complicated, it helps to make some small sketches first, and perhaps a scale drawing that can then be transferred to the wrapping paper. After the design is drawn, cut each section of the design out of the wrapping paper. These will be your templates for cutting the cloth. Don't forget to add ¼″ all around each pattern piece

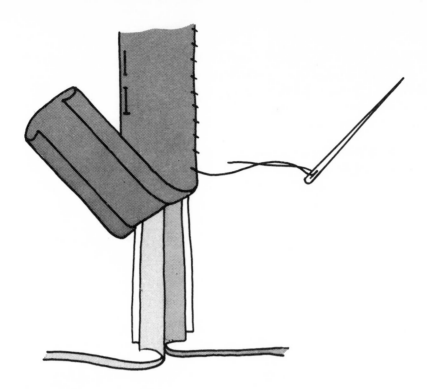

Figure 30 *(Above). To cover the raw edges in a quilted garment, you can use wide bias tape hand-stitched over the seam.*

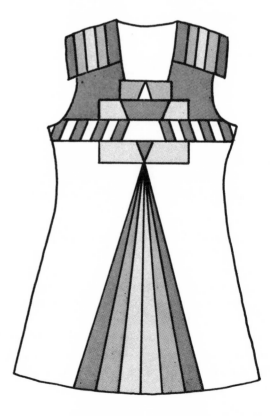

Figure 31. *To put together the entire front or back of a garment, the pattern pieces are traced onto a large piece of paper. A geometric design is drawn on the paper with a ruler or yardstick. The design sections are then cut out and used as templates. The seam allowance is added, the pieces cut out, and the motifs seamed together to form the design.*

for the seam before cutting the cloth. If your design is fairly complicated, number the sections on both your working drawing and on each corresponding template. When all the parts of the pattern have been cut from the cloth, seam them together and finish the garment in the usual way.

Trapunto on Clothing

An entire garment can be trapunto quilted, or spots of trapunto can be used to decorate clothes or accessories.

For quilting a whole garment, the procedure is the same as that given previously in this chapter. Whenever possible, the quilting should be done before the final cutting of the pattern pieces. This is especially important with trapunto because of the excessive amount of "shrinking" during the quilting process, especially with machine work.

For spot trapunto designs, as on the front of a dress, tunic, or blouse, or on collars or cuffs, you can cut the pattern piece out directly if you leave a little extra seam allowance. With spot trapunto, the backing piece needs to be only a few inches larger than the outer edge of the design. After stuffing, the excess backing fabric is trimmed away and the garment lined and finished. In the case of a knit fabric you should not line the garment, but instead trim the backing as neatly as possible.

Finishing

Some of the methods for finishing quilts and hangings can be adapted for clothing. See Chapter 2 for ways of finishing with fringes, ruffles, triangles, etc.

Lining. The best way to finish quilted clothing is with a lining. It hides the mess and gives a professional, finished look to the piece. A lining adds a fourth layer of fabric in addition to the top, filler, and backing.

The lining can be made from one of the fabrics used in the garment or it can be a contrasting fabric. If you wish, you can lavish as much attention on the lining as you did on the outer layer by means of piecing, quilting or appliqué. You can even make the garment reversible. Cut the lining pieces from the same pattern pieces as the outer garment, and seam them together according to the instruction given with the pattern.

Binding. If you intend for the backing to be the lining, you should plan this from the beginning so you can select the proper fabric. Remember to bury the knots in the filler for a smooth finish inside and out. You can bind the raw edges all around with matching or contrasting bias tape. To hide the seams you can hand stitch inch-wide bias tape over the seams as shown earlier.

Hemming. Avoid turning a double hem in quilted fabric, especially if a thick filler has been used. You can zigzag the edge of the garment on the machine and then hem it, or turn up the hem with seam binding.

A Trapunto Design *is spotted on the front of a tunic. The design is machine-stitched on a knit fabric before the tunic is put together.*

The inside *of the tunic front shows how the lining piece has been trimmed close to the stitching line for a neat finish.*

Demonstration   *A Quilted Vest*

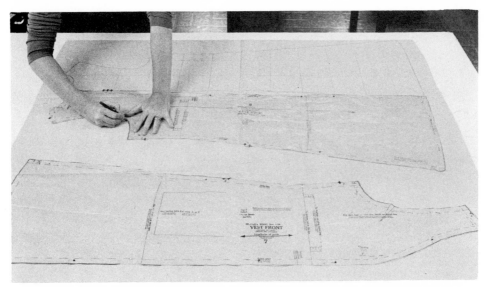

Step 1. *The pattern pieces are placed on the backing material and outlined with pencil. Pattern pieces to be placed on the fold are flipped over to form the whole section. A line corresponding to the straight of the goods is drawn and, using this as a guide, a grid of 3″ squares is drawn right on the cloth to serve as a guide for keeping the patchwork pieces straight. The tissue patterns are unpinned and the sections are roughly cut out.*

Step 2. *The materials are assembled and the patchwork pieces cut out. They are then laid on the pattern using the drawn grid as a placement guide. All of the pieces can be cut and laid out, or sections can be seamed together as soon as a pleasing arrangement is achieved. Any darts should be put into the pieced top before quilting.*

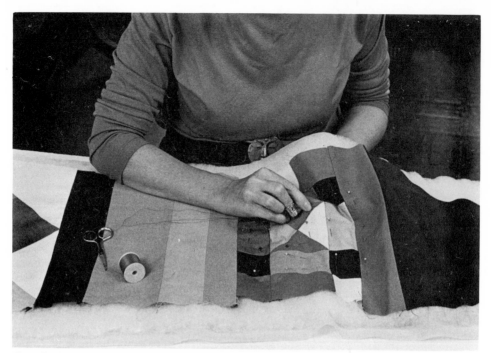

Step 3. *The layers are assembled and pinned together in the area where the quilting is to begin. A simple running stitch is used just inside the seam line of each geometric shape. As the quilting progresses, the fullness is smoothed out to the edges and the pins reinserted in the next area to be quilted.*

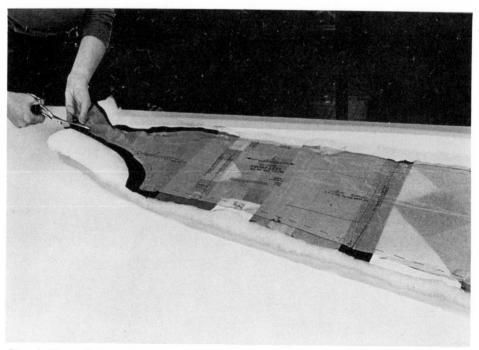

Step 4. *When all the sections have been quilted, the tissue pattern is re-layed, pinned down firmly through all the layers, and the garment sections carefully cut out.*

Step 5. *The garment sections are assembled by following the pattern instructions, and the whole vest is lined according to the instructions given with the pattern.*

Gallery

Shirt. *Patchwork yardage made of pieced triangles is sewn into a colorful shirt from India. No particular attention has been given to the way the design falls on the garment parts. Collection of the author.*

Vest and Skirt by Nina Pellegrini. While giving the appearance of patchwork and appliqué, the pieces have actually been painted with acrylics on muslin and then machine-quilted.

Homage to a Proud People *by Mary Ashby. Squares and rectangles of contrasting cotton fabrics are pieced together in this stunning poncho based on American Indian designs. The piece is not padded, and each square and rectangle is top-stitched to represent a different Indian symbol. Photo by Dennis Hermanson.*

Pieced Skirt *(Right) by Elsa Brown. This simple skirt was made of pieced and plain strips sewn together. The plain area was top-quilted by hand in a running stitch.*

Patchwork Dress *(back view) by Tom and Linda Platt. Silks, satins, damasks, and patterned fabrics have been pieced in strips in this contemporary version of crazy patchwork.*

Hooded Cloak *(Opposite Page) by Nancy J. Clark. This elegant cloak is batik on velvet. The luxurious surface is enhanced by hand-quilting that outlines the batiked shapes. Photo courtesy of the Portland Art Museum, Oregon.*

Tie-Dye and Trapunto Jacket
(Above) by Masako Taka-
hashi. The tie-dye forms were
first outlined with concentric
lines of machine stitching and
then trapunto-quilted.

Tie-dyed and Quilted Boots
(Right) by Letty Shapiro.
These elegant boots could be
called sleeping bags for the
feet. The trapunto-stuffed
channels create a firm
support structure as well as a
relief design. The boots are
stuffed from the inside and
lined. Photo courtesy of the
artist.

Pieced Vest *(Opposite Page)*
by Carol Sarkesian. An ele-
gant vest of pieced velveteen
squares and rectangles. The
pieced strips set in at an angle
are reminiscent of Seminole
Indian work.

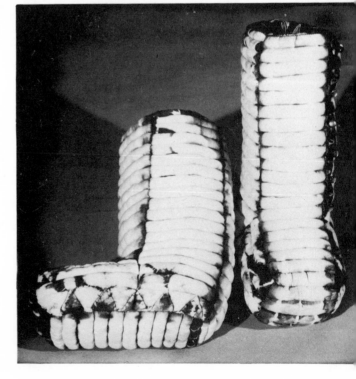

Reversible Jacket *by Sherry Charles. This machine-quilted jacket has sleeves of pieced strips held together with fancy stitching. Photo by Alice Berelson.*

Printed, Painted, and Dyed Fabrics

Dear Robert *by Shirl Salzman, 30" x 45". This machine-quilted wall hanging depicts faces, figures, cars, and hands—all drawn with felt markers on muslin. Some areas have been appliquéd, and beading was added for further embellishment. Photo by Dennis Hermanson.*

$\mathcal{D}$ECORATING OR EMBELLISHING
the surface of fabrics by hand methods of printing, painting, and dyeing has been known for thousands of years. It has not, however, had a long or consistent history of being used in combination with quilting.

Origins

It has been said facetiously that fabric dyeing was discovered when primitive man first sat on a berry. Since no textiles from early cultures have survived, the story must be pieced together from the study of wall paintings, carvings, and other artifacts in use at the time. For example, a variety of stamps found in Mesopotamia dating back 5,000 years ago indicates that techniques of fabric printing were known at that time. From other such indirect evidence, historians have surmised that decorated textiles were in use in Babylonia, Assyria, and Egypt long before the birth of Christ.

Asia and Africa have had long, continuous histories of decorating fabrics with dyes. Block printing, direct painting, stenciling, resist dyeing, tie-dyeing, and combinations of these techniques were all used extensively on both continents, although results differed from one culture to another.

In England and America, chintz, toile, and other printed fabrics were occasionally quilted, but little attempt was made to integrate the quilting patterns with the decorated top. The quilting was usually something that was imposed on the surface as a strictly utilitarian device, either to provide warmth or to extend the life of the cloth.

Contemporary Applications

Perhaps because of the lack of any precise history of the padding and stuffing of painted and printed surfaces, contemporary work in this area seems especially fresh and original. It is a fact that art forms have become more and more sculptural in recent years. This is evident in the manipulated, padded, and shaped canvases of contemporary paintings. The works pictured in this chapter can almost be described as "soft paintings," as indeed they have been by some of their creators. While these imaginative works have been created by professional artists with considerable art training, many of the techniques can be mastered by the average person as well as by children.

The general procedures that follow are not in any way presented as directions to be followed. Rather they are a means of providing additional information and stimulating interest in this area. If you seriously intend to pursue any of these techniques, you should consult additional books or, if possible, take a course in the technique that interests you.

General Procedures

For printing or dyeing, fabrics (usually white) are generally of natural materials. Cotton is the most popular fabric, either muslin or velveteen. Linen,

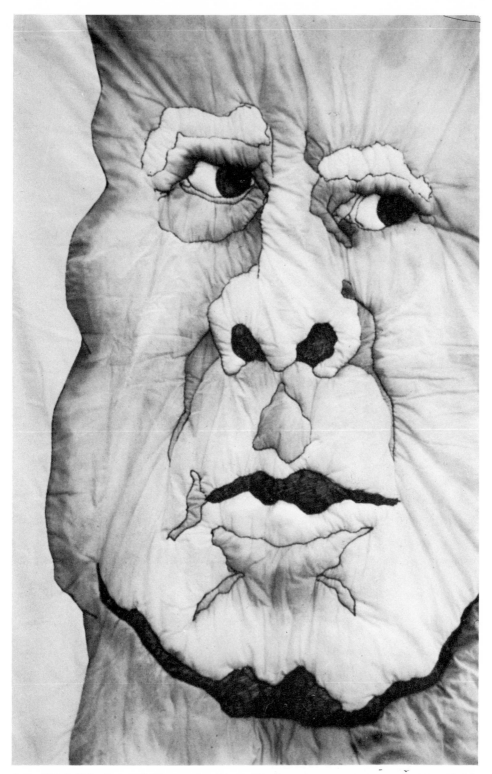

John Mitchell *by Susan Holloway, 6 x 6 feet. The huge face of this former public official was painted directly on cotton fabric with procion dyes. Details were picked up with indelible inks. Finally the face was shaped by stuffing and quilting. Photo courtesy of Sam Moya.*

silk, and rayon are also sometimes used. Polyesters tend to resist dyes, although nylon dyes quite well. The fabric should not have been treated with soil retardants or permanent press chemicals, and it is usually best to wash the fabric first to remove any sizing.

Household dyes can be used for experiments, but they are not fast to sunlight and washing. Fiber-reactive dyes, such as Procion and Dylon, are both fast to light and are washable. For painting, acrylic paint thinned with water, or Versatex textile paints are good. India ink and waterproof felt markers can also be used for drawing fine lines and for filling in areas with color.

After dyeing, the cloth should be set with heat, either by ironing, "baking" in a slow oven for 30 to 60 minutes, or tumbling in a hot clothesdryer. This should be done only after the fabric has dried naturally on a flat surface. In some instances the fabric is again washed, rinsed, and ironed to prepare it for sewing or quilting.

The actual fabric decorating processes fall into two basic categories, and I will briefly describe the basic procedures involved in each one.

Stamping and Printing Methods

These processes involve applying dye or ink by means of a block, stamp, or stencil.

Block Printing. A design is drawn on a wood or linoleum block and the negative space cut away with a gouge. Dye, paint, or ink is then applied with a brayer to the surface of the block, and the prepared block is stamped onto the cloth.

Vegetable Printing. A potato, carrot, turnip, or similar vegetable is cut in half and a design carved on the flat surface. This is then dipped in dye or ink and stamped onto the cloth.

Object Printing. Any "found" object—such as an empty spool, potato masher, leaf, etc.—can be inked and stamped on the cloth. Sponges and rubber erasers can also be cut into various sizes and shapes and then dipped in dye or paint.

Silk Screen. Fine silk cloth is stretched over a wooden frame and the design, adhered to the screen by tusche (a gluelike substance) or by stencil, is printed by forcing color through the exposed areas with a squeegee. A photograph can be transferred by exposing it on photosensitive film, adhering it to the screen, and printing in the usual manner.

Photo Transfer. Images can be transferred from the printed page to cloth with the help of kits sold in hobby shops and art supply stores.

Painting and Dyeing Methods

Dye, ink, or paint is freely applied to cloth by means of brushing or dipping.

Direct Painting. Dyes and textile paints are brushed directly on the cloth, either freely or according to a previously drawn design.

Tie-Dye. Folded, gathered, or pleated cloth is tightly bound at intervals with string or rubber bands and immersed in a dye bath. The binding prevents the dye from penetrating the cloth in those areas, resulting in a sharply defined pattern when the ties are removed.

Batik. Hot wax is applied to the cloth with brushes, stamps, or tjantings (a pen-like tool) and allowed to harden. The cloth is next immersed in a cold dye bath, removed, and allowed to dry. The wax is then removed by ironing or dry cleaning.

Felt Markers. These are excellent for drawing details or when a great deal of control is wanted. The points range from thin to thick, and the waterproof inks come in clear spectrum colors.

Gallery

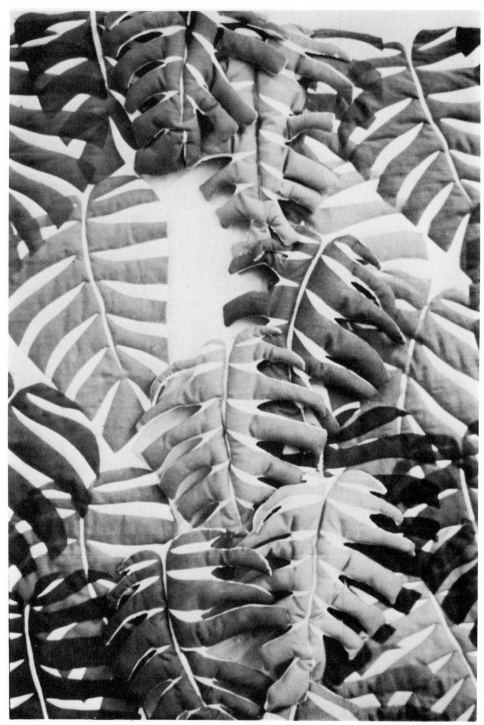

Leaves *by Cindy Blake. Cotton fabric, silkscreen, procion dyes, machine quilting, 4 x 3 feet. The fabric was silkscreened with procion dyes, machine sewn, and then stuffed. First conceived as a fabric, it was eventually converted to a screen for some French doors. The opening in the leaves is for the doorknob. Photo courtesy of Sam Moya.*

Character from Grade One *by Sandy Brown. Cotton fabric, versatex dyes, 30″ x 18″. The artist succeeds in capturing the honest spontaneity of a childhood drawing. The fabric was directly painted with dyes, embroidered for detail, and then machine sewn and stuffed. Photo courtesy of Sam Moya.*

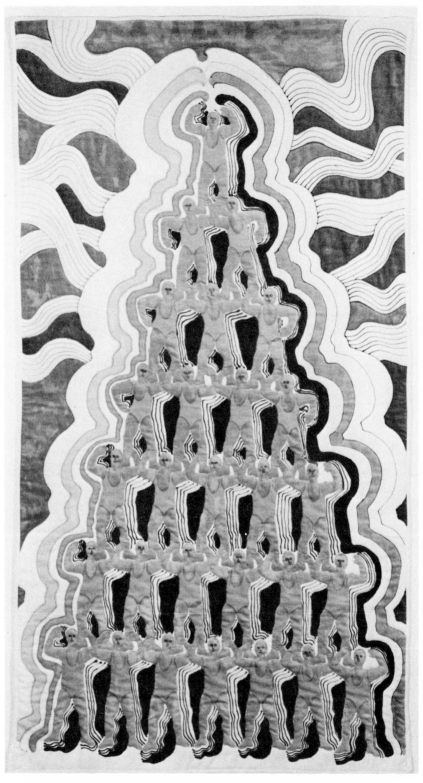

28 Man Pyramid *by Lenore Davis, 34½″ x 62″. Procion dye was applied to cotton velveteen by means of hand stamping and painting, and then the piece was machine-quilted. The lines of stitching echo the painted lines to create a feeling of tension. Photo by Peter Levin.*

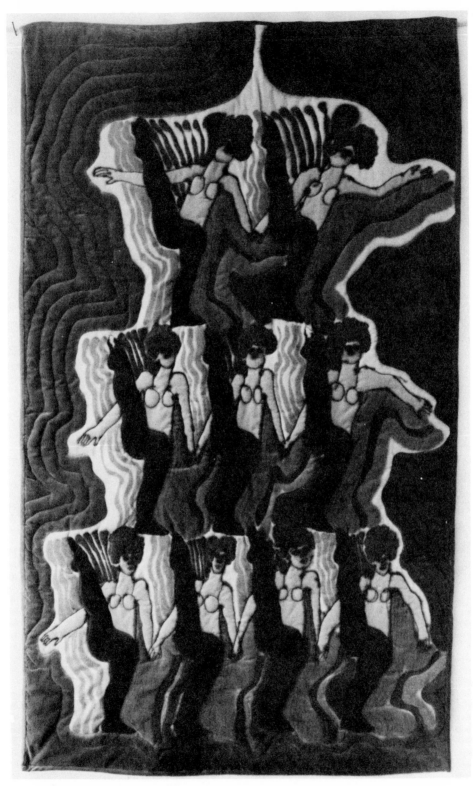

Nine Dancing Girls — Wall Quilt *by Lenore Davis, 32½" x 57". Cotton velveteen is direct-dyed, padded, and trapunto-quilted by machine. The stitching follows the painted lines, creating a feeling of movement. Photo courtesy of the artist.*

Wall Sculpture *by Pat Butler. Batik on cotton, 21" x 31". The cloth was batiked first, then lined, turned to the right side, and quilted by hand. The figures are outlined with stitching and stuffed in a soft bas-relief manner.*

Stripes and Hearts — Wall Quilt *(Right) by Lenore Davis, 32½" x 75". The design is direct-dyed on cotton velveteen, padded and and trapunto-quilted, then machine sewn. Photo courtesy of the artist.*

Being Within *by Kathryn McCardle Lipke, 14" x 24" x 38". Linen gauze has been silk-screened, manipulated into forms, and then stuffed. The geometric screened design creates a tension with the organic stuffed forms. Photo courtesy of the artist.*

Ideas and Design

Coverlet, *English, mid-nineteenth century. This coverlet is made of cut forms silhouetted and sewn to a cotton ground. Courtesy of the Victoria and Albert Museum, London.*

*D*ESIGNING MEANS different things to different people, but essentially it implies a deliberate, planned approach rather than an accidental arrangement of parts. Some people have an innate feel for color, texture, and pattern; others achieve it by hard work involving much trial and error.

Designing

There is no particular right or wrong way to design. What is considered good and bad design is often determined by what is in vogue at the time the object is made. Some designs of 20 years ago seem dated, while others continue to delight. Also, good design is not always the result of years of training.

If you doubt this, think of the beautiful quilts made during the nineteenth century by women with no formal art training or special experience. Whether pieced, appliquéd, or simply stitched, these quilts represent an uninhibited delight in color, pattern, texture, and design. These women took great pride in their quilts, but rarely did they consider themselves artists in the usual sense of the word. Perhaps for this reason the approach was honest and straightforward, not stereotyped or mannered. An entirely intellectual approach, devoid of human response and emotion, would be dry and lackluster. Everyone brings something of his own individual experience to designing, and this results in a personal interpretation. For example, although many standard patchwork patterns were pieced again and again by different women, no two ever looked alike. In this age of standardization and conformity, it is a comforting thought.

The process of designing involves selecting, abstracting, simplifying, and rearranging a series of mental images. These thoughts are then converted into materials that are manipulated until a "just right" arrangement results. This is not as easy as it sounds, and sometimes can be extremely frustrating. Flexibility is the key. You must have the courage to discard a cherished idea that later proves unfeasible, as well as to pursue the most fragile germ of an idea. Often an idea is solidified only when you have begun to work with the materials. Obviously, the design as well as the materials will be dictated by the function of the object. A coat or dress will require a different approach than a hanging or sculpture. Most textile craftsmen are incurable collectors of fabrics and yarns. Having a variety of materials on hand will stimulate your ideas as well as provide a greater range of possibilities.

Your designing abilities will improve if you cultivate the habit of observing and analyzing your surroundings while keeping in mind the basic elements of design.

Line

Lines can be curved or straight, thick or thin, close together or far apart. They can express agitation and motion, or calm and stability. Lines can

An Illustration *from a seventeenth century Ethiopian script of the Four Gospels could serve as a point of departure for a fascinating patchwork and quilted hanging or quilt. The design only needs to be simplified and translated into fabric form. Courtesy of the British Museum.*

create mere surface pattern or the illusion of deep space (as in perspective drawing). Everywhere you look, lines abound in your surroundings: power lines, fences, buildings, television antennas, lettering and calligraphy, tree branches.

Line is especially important in quilting, where often the sole design is a line of stitching. The line must have the power to sustain interest as well as create a feeling of rhythm and balance.

Form

When a line meets itself to enclose a space it creates a form or shape. Forms can be representational or abstract, silhouetted or solid, overlapped or individually spaced. Dominant shapes are considered positive while the space surrounding them is negative. For example, a doughnut is positive space while the hole is negative. Infinite design possibilities can be achieved by playing negative and positive spaces against each other.

Texture

Texture, either actual or implied, is of primary importance in any textile craft. It is the unifying element between the visual and the tactile senses; it prompts one to touch as well as look at an object. Quilting techniques can be used to imply texture when no actual texture exists. When a thick filler has been used between two pieces of smooth cloth, the stitching that holds the layers together indents the cloth to create texture. Trapunto raises the design from the cloth surface to create an embossed texture that depends on the play of light and shadow.

Actual texture can be introduced by the use of textured fabrics, feathers, furs, vinyls, and found objects. Smooth, shiny materials—such as satin, plastic, mylar, etc.—reflect light, while velvets, corduroys, and velours absorb light and take on tonal differences according to the direction of the nap.

Color

The best way to learn about color is by experimenting directly with paint, paper, yarn, or fabric. Some knowledge of color theory is helpful, but ultimately your response is intuitive and emotional rather than intellectual. Colors can be warm or cool, happy or sad, heavy or light. They can express a momentary mood or a lifetime involvement. Many artists go through phases of using one color or combinations of colors exclusively over a period of years until they have exhausted all the possibilities; then they move on to the next phase.

Colors are not always what they appear to be. When viewed against white, a color may appear differently than when viewed against its opposite or another hue. To see what colors do to each other, collect a number of fabric or paper scraps in a variety of colors and place them next to one another. You will see that opposites, such as red and green, tend to intensify one another and seem to vibrate, while related colors are more harmonious.

Color Characteristics. Every color consists of three characteristics: hue, value, and intensity. Hue refers to the pure color name or color family. Colors that cannot be mixed—red, yellow, and blue—are called primary hues. The secondary hues—orange, green, and purple—are produced by combining two of the primary hues. If each of these six hues is mixed with the one next to it on the color wheel, the result is a tertiary color, such as yellow-orange or yellow-green.

Value refers to the lightness or darkness of a color, ranging from white to black. When white is added to a hue, the resulting color is called a tint and is of a higher value, or lighter, than the original color. When black is added to a hue, the resulting color is called a shade and is lower in value, or darker, than the original hue.

Intensity is the brightness or dullness of a hue, and this depends on how much it is grayed. Adding a hue's opposite on the color wheel will gray it, or reduce its intensity.

Rhythm and Balance

Unless the elements of line, form, texture, and color are synthesized into a pleasing relationship, the composition as a whole will be unsuccessful. Rhythm has to do with the way line and form create a feeling of movement or flow and how these separate elements relate to one another. Balance can be symmetrical or asymmetrical, but always implies stability.

Proportion, or the size and relationship of forms to one another, plays an important part in a balanced composition. You can learn a great deal about balance and proportion by studying objects from nature. Notice the striations of a leaf, the arrangement of design elements on a feather, or the wings of a butterfly. The designs seem to happen naturally without forcing or striving, and this is worth aiming for in your own designing. As with color, the ultimate decisions are intuitive and emotional rather than intellectual.

Enlarging a Design

There is a simple way to enlarge your own small sketch, or to enlarge or reduce a design you have found on a greeting card or in a magazine. First, trace the design on a piece of tracing paper, simplifying and adapting as you go. With a ruler, draw a grid of squares of from ½" to 2", depending on the size of the design, right over the drawing as shown in Figure 32. On another piece of paper, draw a similar grid with the same number of squares, but enlarging or reducing the size of the squares according to the final size desired. Then, in each square of the second grid, copy what you see in the corresponding square of the first grid until all the squares are filled in and the design is completed.

Various photographic methods are useful for transferring large designs to paper or cloth. One way is to have a design commercially photostated and blown up to the desired size on paper. Another method is to take a slide of the design and project it in the desired size onto a piece of wrapping paper or fabric that is taped to the wall. You can then transfer the design directly to

Figure 132. *A drawing can be enlarged by drawing a grid of squares over it and transferring the lines in each square to a second grid on which the squares have been enlarged.*

the cloth with pencil or chalk. An opaque projector can also be used to project a picture onto a piece of cloth or paper that is attached to the wall. The image is then traced using the projected image as a guide.

Design Sources

Ideas for designs are all around you; the challenge lies in isolating them or abstracting them from the environment. In the beginning you may be timid about designing from scratch, but whatever you do, do not resort to copying someone else's work. Aside from being dishonest you are cheating yourself as well as the one being copied. By copying, you rob yourself of the experience and fun of developing your own personal expression. You may admire the work of a particular artist, but you cannot start from his point of view. If the technique fascinates you, you can experiment with it until the interpretation is uniquely your own.

Although photographs and reproductions can be invaluable sources of design, again, they are someone else's point of view. If possible, you should observe and draw from actual objects. Keep a notebook to record ideas and sketches for future use. If you don't draw well, you can use simple shapes and symbols, but the object is to sharpen your perception.

Every aspect of your environment and experience is a potential source of design. Perhaps the following categories can help to inspire you and serve as a point of departure.

Materials as Inspiration. Frequently a quilt comes into being because a person has collected a great number of fabric scraps and wants to use them in a creative way. A fabric collection, accumulated over a period of years, can be an invaluable source for beginning.

The Natural Environment. Nature provides endless ideas for designs, whether literal or abstract, organic or inorganic. Take your sketchbook along on a trip to the zoo, a walk in the woods, or a picnic on the beach. Better yet, bring home objects such as pebbles, bark, leaves, and shells for further study. The sun, moon, stars, planets, rain, or fire can be translated symbolically into designs.

Books and Magazines. Designs should be adapted rather than slavishly copied for use in another medium. Art and design books, biology and botany texts, seed catalogs, nature magazines, encyclopedias, and children's books all offer endless possibilities for designs.

Museums. Museums, repositories of man's artistic and technical efforts through the ages, are excellent sources for designs. Actual textile examples, such as embroideries, quilts, or Coptic and Peruvian weavings, can be studied. Motifs from pottery, carvings, paintings, and the like can be interpreted into textile forms. Inspiration can be drawn from entire periods of art, such as Art Deco, Art Nouveau, Pop art, Op art, impressionism, or realism. The works of individual artists such as Paul Klee, Mondrian, Frank Stella, and Robert Indiana can serve as a point of departure for quilting or patchwork.

Design Sources. *The illustrations on these two pages offer a range of design ideas for quilting—children's drawings, American Indian designs, geometric shapes, and gravestone rubbings. See the Bibliography in the back of the book for more information on specific books that offer such designs.*

Symbolism, Mythology, and Religion. Symbols from Indian, early Christian, African, Greek, Roman, and Norse cultures can be used almost without further interpretation. Astrological signs, hex signs, and figures from mythology can be simplified for use as designs. Holidays such as Christmas, Easter, Valentine's Day, and birthdays can stimulate ideas for designs.

Geometric and Free Forms. Pure geometric shapes arrived at mathematically can provide endless patterns for patchwork. Machine parts or household items such as cups and plates can be used as quilting motifs. Folded paper or cloth can be cut freehand to produce shapes for appliqué and quilting.

Fantasy. The extravagant and unrestrained realm of the imagination offers endless possibilities for self expression. Pure fantasy is most evident in the uninhibited art of young children.

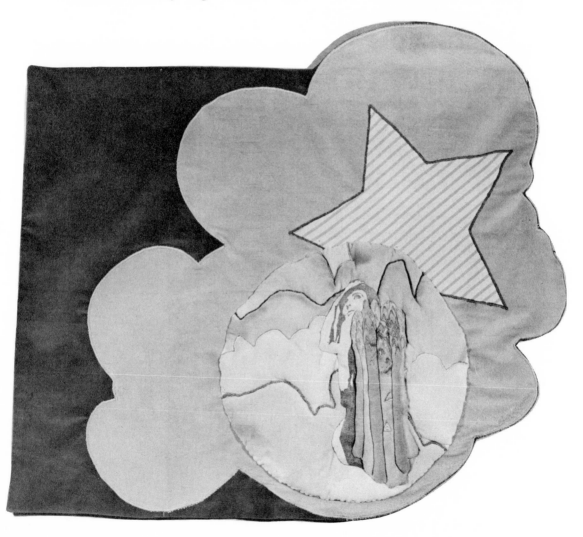

Don't Sit Under the Asparagus Tree *by Joan Blumenbaum, 31" x 27". Cotton velvet, corduroy, linen, and silk yarn. A complex succession of techniques involving silkscreen, dye painting, stitchery, appliqué, and trapunto is utilized in this imaginative hanging. Photo courtesy of the artist.*

Gallery

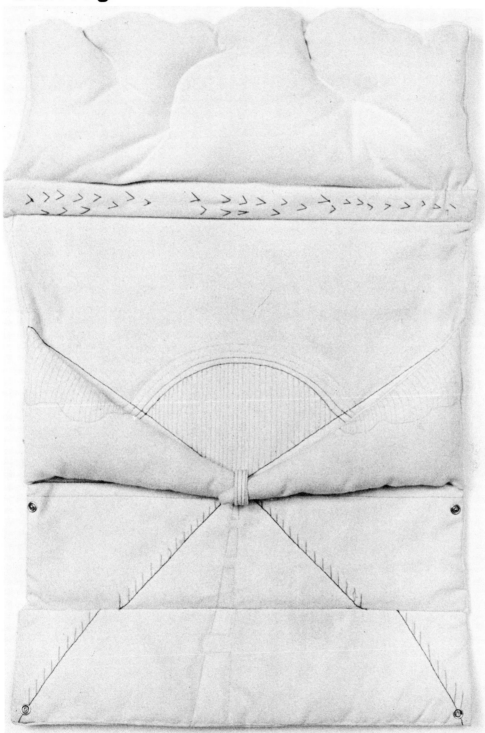

Soft Adjustable Eco-System *by Pat Likos, 14" x 18" closed, 26" x 36" open. This piece, perhaps a soft sculpture, perhaps a movable drawing, was designed to hang on a wall and can be arranged in 12 different positions. It was stitched with colored threads, and parts of the piece were stuffed or trapunto-quilted.*

Plaited Floor Piece *by Letty Shapiro, 3 x 3 feet. Smooth cotton fabric assumes new form and texture when it is stuffed and plaited. Photo courtesy of the artist.*

Butterfly Cape *by Suzanne Derrer. The design of this striking cape-hanging is derived from a butterfly. The design elements have been simplified and adapted to appliqué that is machine quilted. Photo courtesy of the artist.*

Civil War Quilt. *A Civil War veteran, his nerves shattered, began this appliqué and pieced quilt as a therapeutic measure. A wide border depicts appliquéd mounted soldiers and infantrymen. The soldier motif is repeated in the center square, but this time it is over-shadowed by the symbols of peace and love, perhaps indicating a healing. Courtesy of the Shelburne Museum, Inc., Vermont.*

Suppliers List

General Quilting Supplies

Quilts and Other Comforts
5315 W. 38th. Ave.
Denver, Colorado 80212
*Needles, thread, fabric,
batting, frames, hoops.*

Stearns and Foster Co.
Bldg. 34, 11750 Chesterdale Road
Cincinnati, Ohio 45246
Batting and quilt patterns.

Department Stores

Montgomery Ward
By catalog or local store.

Sears, Roebuck & Co.
By catalog or local store.

Dyes

Dharma Trading Co.
P.O. Box 1288
Berkeley, California 94701

Fibrec, Inc.
2815 18th. Street
San Francisco, California 94110

Versatex Paints

Siphon Art Products
Durable Arts Division
74-D Hamilton Drive
Ignacio, California 94947

For British Readers

Ells and Farrier (Beads)
5 Princes Street
London W.1.

Harrods
Brompton Road
London S.W.1.

Liberty
Regent Street
London W.1.

MacCulloch & Wallis Ltd.
25 Dering Street
London W1R OBH

The Needlewoman
146 Regent Street
London W.1.

Useful Information

Embroiderers' Guild
73 Wimpole Street
London W1M 8A

Royal School of Needlework
25 Princes Gate
London S.W. 7.

Bibliography

Books

Brightbill, Dorothy. *Quilting as a Hobby*. New York: Sterling Publishing, 1963.

Carlisle, Lilian Baker. *Pieced Work and Appliqué Quilts at the Shelburne Museum*. Vermont: Shelburne Museum Publications, 1957.

Colby, Avril. *Patchwork*. Newton Centre, Massachusetts: Charles T. Branford, 1970. London: Batsford, 1965.

_____ *Patchwork Quilts*. New York: Charles Scribner's Sons, 1966. London: Batsford, 1965.

_____ *Quilting*. New York: Charles Scribner's Sons, 1971.

Davidson, Mildred. *American Quilts*. Chicago: The Art Institute of Chicago, 1966.

Field, June. *Creative Patchwork*. London: Pitman Publishing, 1974.

Finley, Ruth E. *Old Patchwork Quilts and the Women Who Made Them*. Newton Center, Massachusetts: Charles T. Branford, 1971. London: G. Bell, 1970.

Gonsalves, Alison S. *Quilting and Patchwork*. Menlo Park, California: Sunset Books, 1973.

Green, Sylvia. *Patchwork for Beginners*. New York: Watson-Guptill, 1972. London: Studio Vista, 1971.

Hall, Carrie, and Kretsinger, Rose. *The Romance of the Patchwork Quilt*. New York: Bonanza Books, 1935.

Hinson, Dolores A. *Quilting Manual*. New York: Hearthside Press, Inc., 1966.

Holstein, Jonathan. *The Pieced Quilt*. Greenwich, Connecticut: New York Graphic Society, 1973. Cambridge, England: Patrick Stephens, 1974.

Howard, Constance. *Inspiration for Embroidery*. Newton Centre, Massachusetts: Charles T. Branford, 1967. London: Batsford, 1967.

Ickis, Marguerite. *The Standard Book of Quiltmaking and Collecting*. New York, Dover Publications, 1959.

Johansen, R. Broby. *Body and Clothes*. New York: Van Nostrand Reinhold, 1968.

Jones, Stella M. *Hawaiian Quilts*. Hawaii: Honolulu Academy of Arts Exhibition Catalog.

Laury, Jean Ray. *Quilts and Coverlets*. New York: Van Nostrand Reinhold, 1970.

Lobley, Priscilla. *Your Book of Patchwork*. London: Faber and Faber, 1974.

McKim, Ruby S. *One Hundred and One Patchwork Patterns*. New York: Dover Publications, 1962. London: Constable, 1962.

Marston, Doris. *Patchwork Today*. Newton Centre, Massachusetts: Charles T. Branford, 1969. London: G. Bell, 1969.

_____ *Exploring Patchwork*. Newton Centre, Massachusetts: Charles T. Branford, 1972. London: G. Bell, 1972.

Newark Museum. *Quilts and Counterpanes in The Newark Museum.* New Jersey: the Newark Museum, 1948.

Peto, Florence. *American Quilts and Coverlets.* New York: Chanticleer Press, 1949. London: Max Parrish, 1949.

Proctor, Richard M. *The Principles of Pattern.* New York: Van Nostrand Reinhold, 1969.

Sheras, Evangelina, and Fielding, Diantha. *Appliqué.* New York: Watson-Guptill, 1972. London: Pitman Publishing, 1972.

Short, Erian. *Introducing Quilting.* New York: Charles Scribner's Sons, 1974. London: Batsford, 1974.

Stafford, Carleton, and Bishop, Robert. *America's Quilts and Coverlets.* New York: E. P. Dutton & Co., 1972. London: Studio Vista, 1974.

Strobl-Wohlschlager, Ilse. *Fun with Appliqué & Patchwork.* New York: Watson-Guptill, 1970. London: Batsford, 1970.

Timmins, Alice. *Introducing Patchwork.* New York: Watson-Guptill, 1968. London: Batsford, 1968.

Victoria and Albert Museum. *Notes on Quilting.* London: Her Majesty's Stationery Office, 1960.

Webster, Marie D. *Quilts: Their Story and How to Make Them.* New York: Doubleday, Doran and Co., 1928, and Tudor Publishing Co., 1948.

Wooster, Ann Sargent. *Quiltmaking, the Modern Approach to a Traditional Craft.* New York: Drake Publishers, 1972.

Design Sources

The Dover Pictorial Archives offer a series of books that contain hundreds of illustrations of a variety of pictorial subjects. The following lists some titles that particularly relate to quilting and patchwork. A catalog may be ordered from: Dover Publications, 180 Varick Street, New York, New York 10014.

Christie, Archibald H. *Pattern Design,* 1969.

Edwards, Edward D. *Pattern and Design with Dynamic Symmetry,* 1967.

Enciso, Jorge. *Designs From Pre-Columbian Mexico,* 1971.

_____ *Design Motifs of Ancient Mexico,* 1953.

Gillon, Edmund V. *Geometric Design and Ornament,* 1969.

_____ *Early New England Gravestone Rubbings,* 1966.

Horemis, Spyros. *Patterns and Designs,* 1970.

Williams, Geoffrey. *African Designs,* 1971.

Magazines

Crafts Magazine, 27 Haymarket, London S.W.1.

Creative Needlecraft, Hartree House, Queensway, London W2 4SH.

How To Quilt It (1973, 1974), McCall Pattern Company, 230 Park Avenue, New York, N.Y. 10017.

Quilters Newsletter, 5315 W. 38th Ave., Denver, Colo. 80212. A monthly publication with information on traditional and contemporary quilting and patchwork.

Index

Untitled Coverlet *by Elsa Brown. 65" x 45". Trapunto, patchwork, and tying are all combined in this quilted piece that can be used either as a coverlet or a hammock.*

Cloud Ladies with Sun *by Elsa Brown. Dacron fabric and polyester stuffing, 60" long. This two-part wall sculpture is done in a shadow trapunto technique that uses a translucent top fabric and a black lining. Collection of Mr. and Mrs. Barry F. William.*

Roots and Earth *by Patt Likos. Acrylic on canvas, 36" x 36". The canvas fabric was first machine-quilted and then painted. The result is rather like a "soft painting."*